CLASS REUNION
and
Other Plays

Kermit Frazier

BROADWAY PLAY PUBLISHING INC
New York
www.broadwayplaypublishing.com
info@broadwayplaypublishing.com

CLASS REUNION *and Other Plays*
© Copyright 2022 Kermit Frazier

First edition: September 2022
I S B N: 978-0-88145-946-3
Book design: Marie Donovan
Page make-up: Adobe InDesign
Typeface: Palatino

CONTENTS

DINAH WASHINGTON IS DEAD

DINAH WASHINGTON IS DEAD was first produced at the Milwaukee Repertory Theater (John Dillon, Artistic Director) from April 8-25 April 1982. The cast and creative contributors were:

SARAH...Erma Campbell
RICHARD...Gregory T Daniel

Director... Sharon Ott
Setting....................................Laura Maurer & Tim Thomas
Costumes...Katherine E Duckert
Lighting..Benjamin L White
Properties ....Sandy Struth
Stage Manager ....Cassandra McFatridge
Assistant Stage Managers .... Diane Carlin-Bartel
Jean Anich

CHARACTERS & SETTING

SARAH, *a forty-three-year-old Black woman*
RICHARD, *a twenty-three-year-old Black man*

A three-bedroom rambler in a town near an Air Force Base in West Texas

The Time: Mid-summer, 1971

NOTE ON MUSIC

For performance of copyrighted songs, arrangements or recordings referenced in this play, permission of the copyright owner(s) must be obtained.

(Before the lights come up we hear the voice of Dinah Washington singing, This Bitter Earth. *After the music has played for a while, the lights come up dimly on* SARAH, *a 43-year-old Black woman who is seated on the sofa in the den of her three-bedroom rambler that is located in a town near an Air Force Base in West Texas.)*

(It's a Sunday evening in mid-summer, 1971.)

*(*SARAH *wears a long, bright housecoat and slippers. She sits staring D S and listening to the music. Occasionally, she takes a sip from her gin and tonic, but the bringing of the drink to her lips is the only movement she makes.)*

(The music comes from a tape that's playing on a reel-to-reel tape deck U S of the sofa. The deck is part of an elaborate stereo system, which also includes a receiver, a cassette tape deck, a turntable, and speakers. Also U S is a small bar.)

(The room is filled with furniture, statues, masks, knick-knacks, trinkets, all sorts of things that SARAH *has collected from all over the world. She's a major in the U S Air Force and has traveled extensively.)*

(After a while longer the doorbell rings. SARAH's *only reaction is to turn her head slightly U R toward the exit that leads to the front door. She listens for a moment and then turns her head back, sips her drink, and stares D S. The doorbell rings three more times but Sarah never turns her head again.)*

(Soon there's the sound of the front door opening and closing.)

RICHARD: *(Offstage)* Sarah?

(RICHARD *enters. He's a twenty-three-year-old Black man who is dressed casually.*)

RICHARD: Didn't you hear the doorbell? ...Sarah? ... You left your door unlocked. Not that it makes a difference in this town but still...I could have been anybody.

(SARAH *says nothing.*)

RICHARD: Why are the lights so dim?

(RICHARD *turns up the dimmer on the UR wall.*)

RICHARD: Hey, you awake?

(*Again* SARAH *says nothing.* RICHARD *goes to the stereo and turns the tape off.* SARAH *remains still. Then* RICHARD *goes to US of the sofa and leans over it. HE kisses* SARAH *on the cheek.*)

RICHARD: Hi.

(SARAH *says nothing.*)

RICHARD: Hey, it's me. Richard. Remember Richard?

(SARAH *still says nothing.*)

RICHARD: She ain't sayin' nothing, Richard.... I can see that asshole.... So what you make of it? ...A miracle. It's a goddamn miracle. For once she ain't talkin'.

(RICHARD *laughs but again* SARAH *says nothing.*)

RICHARD: Okay, okay. So I haven't been here in a while. That *is* it, isn't it?

(SARAH *says nothing.*)

RICHARD: All right, just sit there like a zombie. (*Going to the bar*) I'll just drink up all your liquor and eat you outta house and home. Man, am I hungry. (*Seeing a tray of cheese and crackers*) Hey, what kinda cheese is this? (*Taking a bite*) Um-um. Whatever it is, it sure is good. (*He faces U S and looks through the liquor cabinet.*) Listen, you got any of that Scotch I bought a while back? I'd sorta like a change from that gin and tonic tonight.

(During the remainder of RICHARD'*s speech he will make himself a drink and sit facing U S drinking it. At the same time* SARAH *will put her drink down, get up, and slowly walk up to* RICHARD *until she's directly behind him.)*

RICHARD: You know how hot it was today? A hundred and five. That's what happens when there ain't no trees to block the sun. Relentless bastard. Only thing this weather's good for is flying. T-37's and eights out all afternoon. You hear'em? You even been out today? Or did you just sit here basking in your air-conditioned comfort listenin' to ole What's-her-name there?…Shit, I should've gone into pilot training. Would've given me somethin' to do…. Swagger up to your plane like it's your own expensive little toy. Strap yourself in. Check your instruments. Get your clearance. And then take off like a bat outta hell. Soaring over everything instead of clumping through it. Cut right on through all the shit. No hassles. No encumbrances. A fuckin' modern cowboy gallopin' across Texas on his supersonic horse…. Shit, what am I sayin'? In basic training I threw up all over the cockpit in a little ole pussy cat of a T-33. Just couldn't handle it. Besides, we all know what those fuckers are training for. Where they're headed. Hell, this here's a no-win situation as far as I'm concerned, partner. Whichever way you look at it, it's a—

*(*SARAH *touches the back of* RICHARD'*s neck with her hand and he jumps.)*

RICHARD: Jesus, woman, you scared the shit outta me.

*(*SARAH *wraps her arms around* RICHARD *and kisses him passionately. Then she drops her arms.)*

RICHARD: All right, now that's more like it.

(RICHARD *reaches for* SARAH, *but she moves away from him and goes to the stereo system. She turns the Dinah Washington tape back on and goes back to the sofa, where she sits, takes up her drink, and sips it. Then he goes to the stereo and turns the tape off again.*)

SARAH: Turn that back on.

RICHARD: Ah, she speaks.

SARAH: I said turn it back on.

RICHARD: No, I wanna talk.

SARAH: *(Putting down her drink and getting up)* And I wanna hear Dinah Washington.

RICHARD: You've heard this tape a million times.

SARAH: And I'm gonna hear it a million more times. Now turn it back on.

RICHARD: No.

SARAH: *(Going to the stereo)* This is my house, my stereo, my tape, and these are my ears.

(SARAH *turns the tape on and moves D S.* RICHARD *turns it off again.*)

SARAH: You son of a—

RICHARD: What's wrong?

SARAH: You think you can just walk into my house without knocking.

RICHARD: I rang the—

SARAH: Eat up my food.

RICHARD: It's just cheese and—

SARAH: Drink up my liquor.

RICHARD: Hey, now wait a minute. *I* bought the Scotch.

SARAH: I was a present. Remember? You gave it to me. So it's *my* liquor.

(SARAH *moves to turn on the tape, but* RICHARD *grabs her. They tussle with each other a little and then she jerks away from him, which causes him to grab his wrist.*)

RICHARD: *(Wincing in pain)* Ow! Shit!

SARAH: What's the matter with you?

RICHARD: *(Messaging his wrist)* My wrist.

SARAH: What's the matter with your wrist?

RICHARD: I strained it.

SARAH: Just now?

RICHARD: No, not just now dammit.... Ow.

SARAH: *(Eyeing him suspiciously)* It's not strained.

RICHARD: The fuck you know.

SARAH: It didn't seem to be hurtin' a while ago.

RICHARD: And you didn't try to wrench my hand off a while ago.

SARAH: Well, it serves you right.

RICHARD: Shit.

SARAH: Touching my system.

RICHARD: Your system all right.

SARAH: Just keep your hands off it.

RICHARD: Can't even half use it.

SARAH: I do all right for myself.

RICHARD: Half your "specialized" equipment is lying dead in those bottom drawers of yours.

SARAH: Well, I certainly don't need *your* help when it comes to *my* equipment.

(RICHARD *looks pointedly at* SARAH.)

RICHARD: I do all right.

SARAH: What you do is of no interest to me right now.

RICHARD: I can *see* that. *(Massaging his wrist)* Christ.

SARAH: Let me see it.

RICHARD: No. It's all right.

SARAH: Maybe you oughtta wrap it, put some ice on it.

RICHARD: No. Just leave me alone.

SARAH: Suit yourself. *(Slight pause)* So how *did* you strain it?

RICHARD: Playing racquet ball.

SARAH: Racquet ball?

RICHARD: That's right. Racquet ball.

SARAH: Since when?

RICHARD: Since last week… Cutthroat racquet ball.

SARAH: Why?

RICHARD: Why not? …Every day at lunchtime and every afternoon after work. Me and two of my sergeants in supply. Two white, fun-loving, career sergeants…. We try to smash each other. Try to smash the shit outta each other. You know, if I could permanently disable both of them the whole damn supply division would probably crumble. After all, they're the ones who run it. What the hell does a little nigger second lieutenant know anyway? So I've been playing cutthroat racquet ball with them to let'em know who's boss. To keep'em on their toes…. It's so stupid. I get myself in this room, see. And it's like I'm locked in with these two smelly polar bears. And the ball keeps comin', keeps bouncin', faster and faster. And every third time it's mine. Faster and faster. And I try to smash it. Every third time. And I'm thinkin': I've got to get it, I've got to get outta this steamy, smelly hole alive. And their bodies keep shovin' me and I keep dancin' and duckin' and swingin' and smashin'. Faster and faster and faster. Like there's some reason for it all, some reason for me bein' here, for me bein' in this goddam.... *(He calms himself down.)* So that's what I've been doing for the past week. In fact, that's where I'm just coming from. The racquet ball court. Only this time I was there by myself 'cause I wanted to try out some new moves.... New moves all right. Strained my goddam wrist.

(SARAH just looks at him for a moment.)

SARAH: You strained your wrist playing with yourself?

RICHARD: *By* myself. Playing *by* myself.

(RICHARD laughs. SARAH smiles coolly, which causes his laughter to end sooner than it might ordinarily.)

RICHARD: So...what have *you* been doing with yourself?

SARAH: Waiting.

RICHARD: That's a really good way to pass the time.

SARAH: Waiting for you.... Haven't left the house all weekend.

RICHARD: No kidding.

SARAH: No. You see, I didn't wanna miss you, sugar. And I sorta knew that you'd come. That is, I had this strong sense of you comin'. Despite everything.

RICHARD: What do you mean by that?

SARAH: You want something to eat?

RICHARD: What do you mean despite everything?

SARAH: *(Heading for U L exit)* I'll fix you a little something.

RICHARD: It can wait.

SARAH: But I thought you were starving.

RICHARD: Never mind that. What do you—

SARAH: *(Turning back to him)* After all that racquet ball. All that competition. After knocking yourself out all weekend. After straining your wrist and all…. I've got plenty of food here, sugar. Got all kinda goodies for you.

(SARAH starts to go again but RICHARD blocks her way.)

RICHARD: Wait.

(SARAH stops.)

RICHARD: You want me to go?

SARAH: Don't be silly. I said I'd get you something to eat. Don't you wanna eat?

(SARAH tries to step around RICHARD but he blocks her way again.)

RICHARD: Wait a minute… You haven't really been waiting here for me all weekend, have you?

(SARAH kisses RICHARD on the lips and then rubs her hands delicately over his face.)

SARAH: You're beautiful. You know that? Especially around the lips.

RICHARD: *(Smiling)* Thanks.

SARAH: *(Turning from him and stepping D S)* I saw you in the commissary once. I ever tell you that?

RICHARD: No.

SARAH: You were in your khaki uniform. You look really good in uniform. Like something out of a dream I once had a long time ago…. You were at the meat counter. I stood in the aisle behind you with my shopping cart and watched you. You were trying to decide which steak to buy. You were so funny. You kept pickin'em up and weighin'em in your hand and throwin'em down. It was like you didn't know a thing about meat. About any kinda food, really.

Your shopping cart was filled with all this stuff, but I couldn't for the life of me picture what kinda meal you were gonna be able to make with any of it…. I wanted to help you, help you decide. But I didn't. Finally, you just grabbed up a few steaks in frustration, dumped them in your cart, and shoved on.

RICHARD: When did all this happen?

SARAH: You didn't see me.

RICHARD: When?

SARAH: You just didn't see me.

RICHARD: *When?*

(SARAH *just looks at* RICHARD *for a moment.*)

SARAH: Why don't you ever take me out?

RICHARD: Huh?

SARAH: Why don't you ever take me out?

RICHARD: We've been out.

SARAH: When? When have we been out?

RICHARD: What about…what about that party a couple of weeks ago? The one over Colonel Lathan's.

SARAH: Some party.

RICHARD: Well, that was out.

SARAH: Not on the town. Not as a couple on the town. Strolling hand-in-hand because they belonged together, because they had nothing to hide. I don't wanna be some damn attachment dragged along to keep you company just because you don't wanna be among white folks all by yourself.

RICHARD: That's not why I took you?

SARAH: Oh, not?

RICHARD: No.

SARAH: Then what was I there for? Show?

RICHARD: No.

SARAH: Did you run outta phone numbers and finally land on mine?

RICHARD: No.

SARAH: How many numbers do you have anyway?

RICHARD: How many— Look, why are we talking about this? It was two weeks ago, for God's sake. Besides, it was a boring ass party.

SARAH: I know. A perfect description of my only night out with you.

RICHARD: Baby, I came over here to relax, not argue. I thought this was gonna be a relaxing evening.

SARAH: Relax. You wanna relax. Relax from what? What's out there, sugar, that's got you so uptight? *(She goes U S to the window and peers through the blinds.)* I don't see nothing much out there. Except a few ramblers like this one and a long stretch of black sky and a goddam Air Force base splattered across the distance. That's all there is out there. Next to nothing.

RICHARD: Then what's all this crap about wanting to go out, about wanting to do the town? If there ain't nothing out there anyway then what's there to *do*? Why can't you just be content with staying in this elegant mausoleum of yours and let it go at that?

SARAH: This is not a mausoleum.

RICHARD: It might as well be. You bury yourself in here.

SARAH: Because nobody will take me out!

RICHARD: And that's my fault?

SARAH: Yes!

RICHARD: Bullshit!

(RICHARD *turns away from* SARAH, *who just looks at him for a moment.*)

SARAH: You're really slick, aren't you?

RICHARD: *(Turning back to her)* I'm what?

SARAH: You heard me.

RICHARD: You don't know what you're talking about.

SARAH: Oh, yes, I do. I know slickness when I feel it.

RICHARD: Come on, give me a break, will you.

SARAH: You think I don't know, huh? You think I don't know what that oozing slickness feels like. How it begins to cover a man's voice, his attitude. How it begins to shape his excuses, his body, his talk.

RICHARD: I'm not slick.

SARAH: I've been choked by that feeling of slickness many a time before so don't tell me I don't know it when I see it. It's like this film, see. This film that begins to cover your whole body, getting thicker and thicker and thicker until you just gradually disappear.

RICHARD: And what the hell is that supposed to mean? What are you trying to tell me? That I'm not here with you now? 'Cause I am, dammit. I'm looking you right dead in the eye.

SARAH: Uh-huh.

RICHARD: Listen, Ms Sarah, I have not disappeared. You understand me? I have not. I keep myself together. Every last bit of me is still together. So don't be throwing all this crap up in my face.

SARAH: My, my, my. What a nerve I seem to have struck.

RICHARD: That's right, dammit. Shit, you think it's any easier for me? You really think that? 'Cause it's not, dammit. It's *not*. Stuck here in this wasteland. This dry, bareboned of a… *(He lets out a little laugh.)* You know what I did this morning? Just for the hell of it?

SARAH: *(Somewhat hard)* No, I don't.

RICHARD: Drove about sixty miles north of the base. Took my little ole MG up to ninety-five straight on up to where Texas and Oklahoma meet. Turned off the main highway. Stopped at this ole bridge about a mile up the dirt road. Didn't really know where the hell I was. Got outta the car, walked to the stone railing, looked down at where some creek used to be. Just kept looking, staring. Dust. Nothing but dust…. Then I just turned around and leaned against the railing. Watched the fucking sun come up. *(Beginning to pace)* Shit, I hate this place.

SARAH: You'll survive.

RICHARD: I ask for California or Hawaii and they give me this place.

SARAH: At least it's not Vietnam.

RICHARD: I ask for information and they give me supply.

SARAH: Nobody begged you to join the Air Force.

RICHARD: I had to do it.

SARAH: Like hell you did.

RICHARD: I *did*…. College. Air Force ROTC…. A few dudes I knew back in DC are dead now. Army dead. Vietnam dead. Man, was I scared. It was like everybody was being sucked up, sucked in. A fucking whirlpool. Guys being sucked right on out of this world…. And besides, I wanted to be an officer. Just like you, I suppose. I don't like no place but the top. Just like you.

SARAH: And now you're complaining.

RICHARD: I miss things. Things are missing. I miss the trees, the grass, the...water, the people, the—

SARAH: Women.

RICHARD: What? Nah.

SARAH: Back East, or wherever. Back in DC, let's say.

RICHARD: No.

SARAH: Back out of this "wasteland", there'd be more women to choose from.

RICHARD: That's not what I'm talking about.

SARAH: I'd be just another bitch in the crowd.

RICHARD: You're not understanding me.

SARAH: Just another middle-aged bitch.

RICHARD: You're not a bitch.

SARAH: Then take me out.

RICHARD: Jesus.

SARAH: Just the two of us. Take me to dinner, to a movie. Take me somewhere. Prove something.

RICHARD: You act like you've never been on a date before.

SARAH: Those are my conditions.

RICHARD: What conditions?

SARAH: You know what conditions.

(RICHARD *ponders the conditions.*)

RICHARD: All right, I'll take you out. I promise. *(He goes to the bar to make himself a drink.)*

SARAH: When?

RICHARD: Soon.

SARAH: When?

RICHARD: I don't know. Soon.

SARAH: Tomorrow?

RICHARD: No.

SARAH: Tuesday then.

RICHARD: No. Not this week. I've got inventory. It would be too much of a hassle.

SARAH: At night?

RICHARD: Yes, at night. It's a backlog. Christ, what is this?

SARAH: Well, when?

RICHARD: I'll let you know.

(SARAH *just looks at* RICHARD *for a moment.*)

SARAH: You still don't wanna take me out, do you?

RICHARD: Yeah, I do.

SARAH: You think I'd embarrass you.

RICHARD: I never said that.

SARAH: I'm too old. Is that it?

RICHARD: No.

SARAH: It wouldn't be good for your reputation.

RICHARD: No.

SARAH: Poor little Richard. She's the only woman who'll got out with him.

RICHARD: Jesus.

SARAH: *Am* I the only woman who'll go out with you?

RICHARD: All right, next week. Next week we'll got out. For Christ's sake.

(Slight pause)

SARAH: Maybe I remind you too much of your mother. Maybe that's it.

RICHARD: Don't make me laugh.

SARAH: I'm sure I must be her age.

RICHARD: No.

SARAH: I'm *not* her age?

(RICHARD *starts to answer quickly but then catches himself before finally speaking.*)

RICHARD: You don't remind me of her.

SARAH: Really? …Well, to tell you the truth, I've been thinking. Just thinking about it all lately. Sitting here by myself thinking. And what sort of crossed my mind was this—and this is sheer conjecture you understand. But wouldn't it be something if it turned out that I actually knew your mother once upon a time. Back in DC. Back when we were kids growing up in Washington, DC.

RICHARD: You didn't know my mother.

SARAH: That we went to the same school.

RICHARD: You didn't know her.

SARAH: The same Baptist church.

RICHARD: You didn't *know* her.

(SARAH *goes to the bar and makes a drink as she speaks.*)

SARAH: Well…even if we didn't really know each other. What if we had simply passed by each other, brushed by each other, touched each other for just a second? On the street. In the corner grocery store. Down the aisle of some segregated movie house in good ole DC. Way back when. In those pre-Richard days…. What if we'd somehow even tried on the same dresses, fingered the same bras and underwear, moaned and groaned for the same fine young men in our youth, the same hard, smooth bodies? Wouldn't that be something? Wouldn't it be something if you thought I was actually your mother? Wouldn't that help you some? Help make you feel right at home?

RICHARD: You're not my mother.

SARAH: You mean that's not why you like to fuck me?

RICHARD: Goddam you!

(RICHARD *rushes up to* SARAH *and knocks her drink from her hand.*)

RICHARD: How much have you been drinking today?

SARAH: *(Going to the bar to make another drink)* None of your damn business.

RICHARD: 'Cause you must be drunk. That's the only way I'll accept what you just said.

SARAH: Don't make no difference to me how you accept it, sugar.

RICHARD: What are you trying to prove?

SARAH: Nothing, sugar.

RICHARD: I told you I'd take you out next week.

SARAH: How come you didn't take me out last night?

RICHARD: Because I was busy last night.

SARAH: That's what I know.

(*The implications of* SARAH'S *statement soon dawn on* RICHARD.)

RICHARD: Oh.

SARAH: Yeah. Oh.

RICHARD: It was…it was just a going-away party for a cat over in maintenance. Dawson. You know Dawson.

SARAH: No, I don't know Dawson.

RICHARD: Well, he's going to Nam.

SARAH: Too bad.

RICHARD: Leaves Tuesday.

SARAH: How sad.

RICHARD: It was just a little get-together.

SARAH: Didn't sound so small to me.

RICHARD: Well, if you went to all the trouble to call, why the hell didn't you ask to speak to me? I could have invited you over then.

SARAH: I didn't care to come over *then* after having such a nice conversation with Miss What's-her-name on the telephone.

RICHARD: Who?

SARAH: How the hell should I know? Some Airman Ninth Class probably.

RICHARD: Aw, come on, don't be so damn jealous.... And besides, you know officers aren't supposed to fraternize with enlisted folks.

SARAH: Sugar, I've been in this here Air Farce a hell of a lot longer than you have. Sixteen long years. So don't be quoting no obsolete, generally ignored military documents to me.

(RICHARD *says nothing.*)

SARAH: So anyway, what happened? Last night. Or this morning. What really made you zoom on up to the Oklahoma border at ninety-five miles an hour in your good ole MG? What really made you play racquet ball with yourself—excuse me, *by* yourself—this afternoon?...You find out she's not as easy a lay as I am? You mean she didn't fall for your phony moves? You mean she didn't faint over your cocky attitude and your oh so stud-like nature?

RICHARD: All right, now that's enough. That's really enough.... Now I found you. Or don't you remember? Found you asleep on my living room floor at five o'clock in the morning after everybody else had left. It was sorta like you had spent the whole night under a stack of drunk, funky bodies and then all of a sudden, *voilà*, there you were. The last clown to come out of the car at the circus. I found you where I figured Kenny had probably left you when he saw that that particular house party was over for him and he'd better be getting back to his wife. I found you and propped you up and drove you home and got you sober and then spent the next four hours listening to you go on and on about how some white colonel at the hospital was giving you a hard time because he hated Black female officers so much. And then who was it who called and called and kept calling? And who was it who came and came and kept coming? Listening to you babble, watching you drink, putting up with you playing that goddamn Joe Simon forty-five over and over and over again until he coulda sworn that ole Joe was the one you were giving it all to 'cause there sure wasn't nothing coming his way.

SARAH: And who was it who finally did give it to you like she knew you wanted it all along? All those long, sad, sacrificial days you spent over here. Oh, such a magnificent martyr you were.

RICHARD: Don't be so damn self-righteous, woman. You've loved every minute I've spent over here. And right now I'd say that I'm the only person in this whole goddam world keeping you from permanent middle-aged horniness.

(SARAH *slaps* RICHARD *quickly.He raises his hand to slap her back but then stops himself. She moves away from him.*)

(*Slight pause*)

RICHARD: Look, Sarah, I...I didn't really mean it the way it sounded.... I'm sorry. I'm really sorry.

SARAH: I know. Believe me, I really know.

(RICHARD *moves to* SARAH, *but she backs away quickly.*)

SARAH: No. No, no, no. I am not poor…. I'm not
poor…. I'm not poor, you know. *(She begins to move
around the room, touching and handling her possessions.)*
Just look around you. Whirl yourself around this room.
Let your eyes, let your hands glide over a few things
here. Feel the texture, the temperature, the weight of
things. Feel the real significance of everything here….
And check out where things are from. Thailand, Hong
Kong, Japan. Ah, those Asian men. And this is Hawaii.
Hickam Air Force Base. What a tour of duty. Maybe
you'll get there yet. Just keep trying. And here we
have Germany. Wood inlays from Stuttgart. A famous
Hofbräuhaus stein from Munich. Expensive Hummel
ware from Frankfurt. And then there's Greece. Dirt
cheap clay wine goblets from Crete. Handmade little
trinkets from the Plaka district in Athens. And of
course, Africa. Mother Africa. Masks, statues, ivory.
Our heritage and sweat on display…. Take the tour.
Survey the entire house. Refresh your memory.
Reacquaint yourself with how much of the world is
in this house. Just check out for yourself again how
unpoor I am.

RICHARD: Sarah, I—

SARAH: No words from you, buster. Not now!

*(RICHARD stands tensely. After a moment SARAH moves
on.)*

SARAH: My mother still cleans up after white folks.
Did you know that? Followed them right on out to the
suburbs still cleaning up after them. Takes something
like three buses but she still goes. You see, they need
her. And besides, everybody's gotta live. But I won't
be …. And my sister, she's still got this low-level
government job, even though she's been working for
years, ever since her husband left her. Things take
time, she always says, never half believing it. Scars,

promotions. Time. But I won't…. And her kids, Well,
little niecie's on welfare now 'cause she's got two
kids of her own and little nephew's a security guard
somewhere, some damn where. I don't know. He's the
only one who ever writes me for money. The rest of'em
call. Call collect. It's always so good to be stationed
out of the country. You see, he's got all these deals,
all these plans in his head. He wants so much. And I
do help out as much as I can. I really do. God knows
I do. But I won't be held…completely responsible…. I
am not a bottomless pit. I am not an insensitive bitch.
I am not a Black woman chasing shadows. I am not—I
am…. I am a forty-three-year-old nurse/anesthetist.
I am a major in the goddam United States Air Force.
I have seen more of the world than that whole
neighborhood I stumbled out of will ever see in their
collective lives. So I am rich. Do you hear me? Rich as
can be. Rich and mature and independent. So what the
hell did I ever need from you anyway? (*Slight pause.
Facing away from* RICHARD) Turn my Dinah Washington
tape back on.

RICHARD: Sarah, please, let me stay.

SARAH: (*Still not looking at him*) No.

(RICHARD *goes to* SARAH *and embraces her from behind.
She feels the warmth of his touch but tries to steal herself
against it.*)

RICHARD: Please. I don't wanna go back out there
tonight. Not alone.

SARAH: I know.

(RICHARD *kisses Sarah tenderly on the neck. She rubs his
arms, almost involuntarily.*)

RICHARD: Then why can't we—

SARAH: (*Pulling away quickly*) No.

(Still behind SARAH, RICHARD *looks longingly at her for a moment. Then he touches her again gently. But when she stiffens, he drops his arm.)*

(He goes slowly to the tape deck and turns on the tape. The song, This Bitter Earth, *continues. Then he looks around at many of the objects* SARAH *had pointed out to him before, even touching some of them as he works his way to the front door. He stops at the door as though to say something more, but then he simply leaves.)*

(When SARAH *hears the front door close she shudders, tears welling in her eyes. But she doesn't turn to the door.)*

(The music rises as the lights fade to black.)

END OF PLAY

CLASS REUNION

CLASS REUNION was first produced at the Ensemble Studio Theatre (Curt Dempster, Artistic Director) in New York, in Marathon 1982. The cast and creative contributors were:

ERNIE .... Mac Randall
GLORIA .... Stephanie Rita Berry
TOM.. Carl Lumbly

Director .... Madeleine Thornton-Sherwood
Scenic design .... Brian Martin & Dana Hasson
Costume design .... Madeline Cohen
Lighting design .... Richard Lund
Sound design ....Gary Harris
Production Supervisor ....David S Rosenak
Production Stage Manager ....Richard Heeger

CHARACTERS & SETTING

Ernie, *Black man, 20s*
Gloria, *Black woman, 20s*
Tom, *Black man, 20s*

A living space in an American city

The Time: The 1980s—before social media, cell phones, or computers

(*The lights come up on* ERNIE *and* GLORIA, *a Black man and a Black woman respectively who are in their twenties. They sit in chairs, facing downstage. There is nothing else in the space.*)

(*A long, long silence*)

GLORIA: You said he was comin'.

ERNIE: I know I said he was comin'.

(*Slight pause*)

GLORIA: So where is he?

ERNIE: On his way.

(*Slight pause*)

GLORIA: How do you know he's on his way?

ERNIE: 'Cause he ain't here yet.

(*Pause*)

GLORIA: Maybe he's not comin'.

ERNIE: He'll be here.

GLORIA: Maybe he lied.

ERNIE: What would he do that?

GLORIA: I don't know. To trip you up maybe. Bend you outta shape.

ERNIE: I ain't bent outta shape.

(*Slight pause*)

GLORIA: To laugh at you then.

ERNIE: Why would he wanna laugh at me?

GLORIA: 'Cause you're you.

ERNIE: Just stow it, baby, okay?

(Slight pause)

(GLORIA laughs.)

GLORIA: He's probably home right now laughin' at you.

ERNIE: Now look—

GLORIA: I can just see him right now fallin' all over hisself laughin' at you.

ERNIE: I'll fall all over you in a minute.

GLORIA: *(Laughter stopping)* You and what army?

ERNIE: You beginnin' to get on my nerves.

GLORIA: I'm just tryin' to be of some assistance here, that's all.

ERNIE: I don't need any—

GLORIA: Help you figure this out, that's all.

ERNIE: There ain't nothin' to figure out.

GLORIA: I mean like he's got your address, don't he?

ERNIE: Of course, he's got the damn address. What do you think I am? Stupid? I gave him the goddam address.

GLORIA: All right, all right. *(Pause)* So that explains why he's not comin'.

ERNIE: He'll be here dammit! *(Slight pause)* What explains why he's not comin'?

GLORIA: The fact that he's got your address.

ERNIE: Oh, really?

GLORIA: Yeah.

ERNIE: *(Incredulous)* That makes a hell of a lotta sense.

GLORIA: Makes sense to me.

(Slight pause)

ERNIE: So what is it? What's the explanation?

GLORIA: All right. He knows this can't be no palace you're livin' in here. Not with this address. That is, if he knows anything about this town, which he must do 'cause he did grow up here right along with the rest of us. And although I didn't know him in high school I'm sure he—

ERNIE: What do you mean you didn't know him?

GLORIA: Just what I said. I didn't know him. In fact, neither did you really.

ERNIE: Like hell I didn't. He was president of the Student Council, for God's sake. *Everybody* knew him.

GLORIA: Not to speak to. Not to be friends with. Not to say, hey, why don't you slide on over to my place for a while? Drink a few, smoke a few, rap a little, tell some lies. Not that well. You didn't know him all that well. And neither did I. I mean we ain't in his class. Why can't you accept that fact? We ain't in his class.

ERNIE: So what? *(Unthinkingly)* We all black under the skin, ain't we?

GLORIA: What?

ERNIE: Never mind.

GLORIA: What did you just say?

ERNIE: Forget it.

(Slight pause)

GLORIA: Well, anyway, the point I was tryin' to make is he ain't gonna come to this dump if he can help it. Not to see nobody he just happened to bump into on the street after all these—

ERNIE: We didn't just bump—

GLORIA: Which don't really matter anyway 'cause he never even knew him in the first place.

(Pause)

ERNIE: He doesn't think this place is a dump.

GLORIA: How do you know?

ERNIE: I just know.

GLORIA: He's got the address, don't he?

ERNIE: Yes. How many times I gotta—

GLORIA: Then I stick to my original remarks…. Do *you* have *his* address?

ERNIE: No.

GLORIA: And why not?

ERNIE: He didn't give it to me.

GLORIA: See? …And do you know why he didn't give it to you?

ERNIE: No. But I've got the strangest feelin' I'm gonna be findin' out real soon.

GLORIA: 'Cause he didn't want you callin' him, that's why. Didn't want you pickin' up the ole telephone and dialin' his number, disturbin' him from his important business with his high-class friends, askin' him if he just happened to have forgot he was supposed to come over here a whole goddam hour ago.

(Slight pause)

ERNIE: I could look it up.

GLORIA: What?

ERNIE: His number. I could look up his number.

GLORIA: How? You said he didn't live here no more. That he was just passing through on his way to business school or somethin'.

ERNIE: Graduate school in business. There's a big difference between business school and graduate school in business.

GLORIA: What's the difference?

ERNIE: Graduate school in business means you already finished college once.

GLORIA: Well, good for him.

ERNIE: Yes, indeed. He's on his way to bein' one of those corporate executives, one of those manipulators of money and men. College was just a small step, he said. There's more important things down the line, more significant things waitin' for him just over the near horizon.

GLORIA: Yeah, well, none of that there hearsay information sheds any light on the telephone number situation.

ERNIE: He's stayin' with his parents while he's in town. I could just look in the ole telephone book under his father's name, suck the ole telephone number temporarily into my memory bank, and then call the motherfucker up.

GLORIA: And how do you happen to know his father's name?

ERNIE: 'Cause I happen to know he's a junior. 'Cause I happen to remember a hell of a lot more things about him that you do. Now will you just shut up and let me wait in peace.

(Pause)

GLORIA: So call him up.

ERNIE: No.

GLORIA: Why not?

ERNIE: 'Cause he's on his way. Which means that it would be a waste of time and energy to call him up, Gloria.

(*Slight pause*)

GLORIA: You always so damn sure of yourself, ain't you? So damn sure. Why is it that a man who's always so damn sure of hisself can be so damn wrong most of the time? What is that? Will you answer that question for me?

(ERNIE *just stares at* GLORIA *for a moment.*)

ERNIE: I know he's gotta show 'cause we made a special deal.

GLORIA: What special deal?

ERNIE: Never mind what special deal.

GLORIA: Bullshit.

ERNIE: If you say so.

GLORIA: I don't believe it.

ERNIE: Good.

GLORIA: I don't believe a word of it.

ERNIE: Good, good. Then you don't have to be thinkin' on it no more, now do you?

(*Pause*)

GLORIA: What sorta special deal?

ERNIE: Just forget it, okay? There ain't no deal. So forget it. It'll just be one small-assed reunion, that's all. Just a few drinks or whatever with an ole partner from high school, that's all. No special deals.

GLORIA: Is he comin' here to cop? Is he "comin' slummin'" just to buy some shit? Are you dealing again?

ERNIE: No.

GLORIA: Then what is it?

ERNIE: He wants to— We're gonna— Let's just say that he needs me, okay?

GLORIA: Oh, Mr Big Time, eh?

ERNIE: That's right.

GLORIA: *He* needs *you.*

ERNIE: Yeah.

GLORIA: And I suppose you *don't* need him.

ERNIE: I ain't say that.

GLORIA: And what's in it for me?

ERNIE: Just wait and see.

GLORIA: *(Getting up)* No, I don't think so.

ERNIE: Where you goin'?

GLORIA: Out.

ERNIE: What for?

GLORIA: Look, I ain't lettin' no silver-spooned, college grad Negro control my life just 'cause we might happen to have one or two memories in common.

ERNIE: But don't you wanna see him?

GLORIA: No, I don't. *(She starts to leave.)*

ERNIE: He wants to see you.

(GLORIA turns back to ERNIE.)

GLORIA: He said that?

ERNIE: Yep. Said he was really looking forward to seeing you again.

GLORIA: What do you mean again?

ERNIE: He remembers you. Remembers you well.

GLORIA: He said that to you?

ERNIE: Yep.

GLORIA: Then he was lyin' 'cause I don't even know him.

ERNIE: He knows you.

GLORIA: Shit.

ERNIE: He recognized your picture.

GLORIA: What picture?

ERNIE: The one I showed him.

GLORIA: You showed him a picture of me?

ERNIE: Yep.

GLORIA: When?

ERNIE: The last time he was here.

GLORIA: He was here before?

ERNIE: Yeah.

GLORIA: When?

ERNIE: Earlier this week.

GLORIA: He was here earlier this week?

ERNIE: Yeah.

GLORIA: You didn't tell me he was here earlier this week.

ERNIE: Slipped my mind.

GLORIA: Jesus, Ernie.

ERNIE: Yes, indeedy. Gave me a lift home in his brand new red Corvette. Yeah. What a fucking beautiful machine. His parents gave it to him for his graduation from college, I think he said. Yeah. That's what he said. Brought me right up to the ole curb, to the ole door in that graduation present of his. Folks lookin', cuttin' and twistin' they heads and eyes to see us, wonderin' who this nigga was I knew so well.

GLORIA: You don't know him well.

ERNIE: Maybe not. But some folks was probably thinkin' it just the same. And that counts for somethin'.

GLORIA: You never told me that.

ERNIE: Nevertheless, it's true.

GLORIA: You never told me he was here before.

ERNIE: Yes, indeedy do.

GLORIA: You told me you just bumped into him on the street.

ERNIE: Me and him, just dealin' away.

GLORIA: That he hardly even remembered you at first.

ERNIE: *(An outburst)* Well, he should have remembered dammit! He should have!

(Slight pause)

GLORIA: Ernie, what's goin'—

ERNIE: So you see, he *does* know that I don't live in no high-class neighborhood, that I don't live in no palace. But it don't matter, see, 'cause this deal's got nothing to do with palaces.

GLORIA: How many other times he come snoopin' around here without me knowin' it?

ERNIE: He ain't come snoopin'.

GLORIA: How many other times?

ERNIE: None.

GLORIA: Uh-huh. Well, you can just deal away, Mr. Small Time. Deal right on away. Have yourself an honest-to-goodness ball dealin'. I've got better things to do with my time. *(She starts to leave again.)*

ERNIE: Where you goin'?

GLORIA: Wherever I choose.

ERNIE: When you comin' back?

GLORIA: Hopefully, long after what's-his-name has gone. If he ever shows.

ERNIE: Why don't you wait just a few more minutes? He should be here any minute now.

(GLORIA *just stares at* ERNIE *for a moment.*)

GLORIA: You know what I think? This is just another one of your mind trips, just another game you runnin' down to try and keep me from goin' out tonight.... You ain't waitin' for no Tom. You don't even know no Tom. Never in your life have you known a Tom. There ain't nobody comin'.

(GLORIA *exits.* ERNIE *sits in silence for a moment. Then he closes his eyes slowly. The lights fade out on him and a spotlight comes up on* TOM, *a Black man in his twenties.*)

TOM: When I'm in my car it's like being in my own private little world. White interior, bucket seats, bossed-out stereo C D player. A sleek, smooth, air-conditioned sound system on wheels. My own music and my own space. I was born to make my own music and my own space. Slicing through the hot, sticky, funky air with the knife-edge of my privileged life. Carving out a chunk of territory for myself that no one would dare lay claim to, dare even enter without my permission. I can ride through the streets of this or any other town and feel as safe and secure and insulated as I did on that college campus. Me strutting among all those white folks, on top and very, very neat and clean, money in my pockets, beautiful women hovering like bees around honey, and a rich, bright future waiting for me just over the near horizon.... A glider through life. That's me. That's my continual aim. That's my ever-growing claim to fame. A strong, solid, sophisticated glider through life.

(TOM *smiles. The spotlight fades out on him, and the lights come up on* ERNIE, *who is also smiling, still sitting with his eyes closed. Then* ERNIE *opens his eyes, and* TOM *enters, looking around the space as though he's never seen it before. Finally,* TOM *nods his head.)*

TOM: Yeah, this will do just fine.

ERNIE: You're late.

TOM: What?

ERNIE: You're late.

TOM: I don't think so.

ERNIE: It's ten o'clock.

TOM: We said ten.

ERNIE: *I* didn't say ten.

TOM: You said it to me.

ERNIE: I said nine.

*(*TOM *smiles.)*

TOM: Then one of us is misinformed, isn't he?

*(*ERNIE *glares at* TOM *for a moment. Then he gets up and begins walking around nervously.)*

ERNIE: Yeah, yeah. Shit, it don't matter all that much anyway. Maybe it's just as well.

TOM: Why? What's up?

ERNIE: Nothin'.

TOM: You're not getting cold feet, are you?

ERNIE: Shit, no.

TOM: Then what's the problem? Why are you so nervous?

ERNIE: I ain't nervous.

TOM: If anyone's going to be nervous it should be me.

ERNIE: Oh, yeah? And why is that?

TOM: I've got more at stake.

ERNIE: Like hell you do. You ain't that much different than me.

TOM: Then why the deal?

ERNIE: It's *your* deal.

TOM: You've agreed to it.

ERNIE: Yeah, because I... That is, you... Anyway, I've got a right to be just as nervous as you.

TOM: *(Smiling)* But I'm not nervous.

(Slight pause)

ERNIE: Uh...listen. There's somethin' I haven't told you yet.

TOM: What?

ERNIE: I hope it won't make too much of a difference.

TOM: What is it?

ERNIE: I tried to keep her here so I could explain everythin' with the real McCoy present.

TOM: Who?

ERNIE: But then she left.

TOM: *Who?*

ERNIE: I mean, she thinks that all I do is—

TOM: Who the hell are you talking about?

ERNIE: *(Hesitantly)* Gloria.

TOM: Who's Gloria?

(ERNIE says nothing.)

TOM: I thought this was going to be one-for-one.

ERNIE: It is.

TOM: Are you married?

ERNIE: No, no. She just sorta lives here, that's all.

(TOM simply stares at ERNIE.)

ERNIE: All right, she *does* live here.

TOM: I see…. And she doesn't know.

ERNIE: No, not yet. You see, she'd never believe me. That's why I was sorta hopin' that *you'd* explain it to her.

TOM: Me?

ERNIE: Yeah. As a matter of fact, I'm almost positive you'd be able to explain it to her. Explain it to her real good. I mean, I know you got to be much better at explanations and shit than me. That's why I agreed in the first— And it's not like she's a stranger or somethin'. I mean, she *did* go to the same high school as we did. And at the same time, too. Here, look. *(He takes out his wallet and begins fumbling with it.)* I've got a picture of her in here somewhere…. Shit, the last time we talked I got so flipped out over this fuckin' crazy-assed idea of yours that I clean forgot about old Gloria. But I know it won't make that much of a difference. Might even help. Make you feel more at home and shit. Where the hell's that— *(Finding the picture)* Here it is.

(ERNIE, *giving the picture to* TOM)

ERNIE: Remember her?

*(*TOM *studies the picture.)*

TOM: I…I'm not sure.

ERNIE: She remembers you.

TOM: She does?

ERNIE: Yeah. Remembered you right off. Hell, why shouldn't she? Student Council and all that stuff. It's just that she had other plans tonight and couldn't wait no longer. Didn't have anything to do with you.

TOM: *(Studying the picture again)* But what if she won't go along?

ERNIE: She'll go along. She's the adventuresome type. Besides, it's not like it's permanent or anything, right?

(TOM *thinks for a moment.*)

TOM: All right.

ERNIE: Hey, man, outta sight.

TOM: (*Holding out his hand*) The keys.

ERNIE: (*Holding out his hand*) Can I have the picture back? My way of keepin' in touch.

(TOM *returns* GLORIA's *picture.*)

TOM: (*Again holding out his hand*) The keys.

ERNIE: Yours first.

TOM: What's the matter? Don't you trust me?

ERNIE: Trust you? Are you kiddin'? A fine brother like you? A good ole fellow alum from Central High? (*Slipping into memory*) A blood I used to follow with my eyes all over the school whenever I got the chance. A cat whose chair I used to sit in after he'd warmed it up for me when we took history back to back in room 213. A dude I've even dreamt about from time to time. (*Back to* TOM) Man, I trust you like you were my own brother. I trust you just as much as you trust me.

(TOM *looks at* ERNIE *for a moment. Then he takes a set of keys out of his pocket, hesitates, and then tosses them to* ERNIE. ERNIE *catches them and shakes them in his hand.*)

ERNIE: Yes, indeedy do. They sure got a nice ring to them.

TOM: (*Holding out his hand*) Yours.

ERNIE: (*Smiling*) Uh-uh.

TOM: What?

ERNIE: Not yet.

TOM: (*Stepping toward* ERNIE) Why you—

ERNIE: Wait, wait. First you gotta tell me why.

TOM: I told you before not to ask for an explanation.

ERNIE: I know. But now I think I want one. Just for the record.

TOM: For the—

(TOM *makes a couple of moves to grab* ERNIE, *but* ERNIE *dodges him each time.*)

TOM: Look, I could just walk right out on this, you know.

ERNIE: I know.

TOM: I don't have to be doing you this…favor.

ERNIE: 'Course not.

TOM: I could just choose somebody else. Choose somebody else at…random. Leave you to rot in this goddam place.

(ERNIE *says nothing.*)

TOM: Look, *I'm* the one playing the good Samaritan here, the one making the sacrifices. *I'm* the one who's going back to college, who's going places. I don't have to be doing this. I don't have to be fucking doing this. I could just fucking leave right now!

(ERNIE *glares at* TOM *for a moment. Then he tosses* TOM's *keys back to him.*)

ERNIE: So leave.

(TOM *stares at his keys for a long moment. Then he looks at* ERNIE.)

TOM: You. (*Slight pause*) One morning, away at college, in my very first year, I woke up suddenly at about four A M. Just popped my eyes open at four A M. My roommate was still sleeping in his part of the room. Still curled up in his blanket and secure in his part of the room. I got up and went to the window and looked

out onto the campus. No one in sight. No sounds to
speak of. So with my mind I pushed myself out of the
window and onto the grass. At first the dampness on
my bare feet chilled me. But soon it began to arouse
me, to make me feel potent, alive. In my head I raced
up and down the campus, tumbling and rolling
around and around in the grass, every inch of my
skin becoming wet and potent and very, very alive. It
was so exhilarating. And after a while, when I finally
came down, I thought how, at the height of the day,
with the grass sucked dry by the sun, with hundreds
of students milling around, I felt nothing. Nothing at
all. *(Slight pause)* I turned from the window and looked
at my roommate again. I stared at him for quite some
time. I bored a hole in the center of his blond head with
my sizzling stares. Then I climbed through that hole
and walked around inside of his head. And through
his eyes I could see the window, I could see books and
clothes, I could see all around my side of the room.
But I couldn't see *me*. I had disappeared without a
trace. It was one hell of a surprise. *(Slight pause)* Several
weeks later, very early one morning again, walking
the campus alone, walking for real this time, a campus
security guard pulled up in his shiny black and white
car and stopped me…. You see, he thought I was
trespassing.

(TOM *looks directly at* ERNIE *for the first time since the
opening moment of his explanation.*)

TOM: He thought, in fact, that I was you. And for
one sharp, lightening, crazy second I felt that kind of
orgasmic exhilaration that I'd felt in my head weeks
before.

(Pause)

(TOM *tosses his keys back to* ERNIE *and then holds out his
hand.*)

TOM: The keys, please.

(ERNIE *takes a set of keys out of his pocket and weighs them in one hand as he weighs* TOM's *keys in the other. Then he tosses his keys to* TOM, *who catches them. They stand looking at each other for a moment. Then* ERNIE *exits.*)

(TOM *breathes a sigh of relief, puts the keys in his pocket, and walks around the space. Then he sits down in the chair* ERNIE *had been sitting in. He closes his eyes and massages his temples. The lights fade out on him and a spotlight comes up on* ERNIE.)

ERNIE: You live on the border, on the edge of things your whole life, keepin' your mind and your innermost feelings in check as much as you possibly can 'cause folks don't want no slippage, see, no pots boilin' over. Scares them too much. I mean, that's when they be draggin' out the extra cages and shit and you want as little of those kinds of bars in your life as is absolutely necessary. Still, there's this tightrope, see. This tightrope. And it's way too thin for your big-assed feet. So you just know you gotta be tumblin' now and again. And that's where your ole lady comes in. And of course you should know it ain't no one-way street I'm talkin' about here. I mean like you gotta be a net for her, too. Alls I'm saying is that she does make herself available. Does help out. That is, she *can* help out. Or rather she *might*.... Anyway, I just wanted to give you somethin' to be thinkin' on while you're figurin' out how to get next to her, how to keep her interested, satisfied.

(*The spotlight fades out on* ERNIE *and the lights come up on* TOM, *who opens his eyes quickly. At that moment* GLORIA *enters. She glares at* TOM. *Then she walks downstage in full view of him. He studies her for a moment and then smiles.*)

TOM: Yes.

GLORIA: Who are you?

TOM: You don't remember me?

GLORIA: No… Where's Ernie?

TOM: High school. Remember?

GLORIA: No, I don't. Where's Ernie?

TOM: He went out.

GLORIA: Why?

TOM: I don't know.

GLORIA: You mean to tell me he just went out for no special reason and left you here alone?

TOM: I can take care of myself.

GLORIA: And what about this place? Who'll take care of it? How's he know you won't rob us blind while he's out?

TOM: Because he trusts me like a brother.

GLORIA: Well, I don't, "brother."

TOM: But you weren't here when he left, were you? And now that you're back I can't really rob you of anything, can I?

GLORIA: Damn straight you can't. *(Slight pause)* Why you lookin' at me like that?

TOM: You must remember me.

GLORIA: Why must I remember you?

TOM: Because we were in high school together. All of us. You, me, Ernie.

GLORIA: Now look, buster, there musta been a good two thousand folks in that high school. How the hell am I supposed to remember every goddam person that went there? What was so damn special about you that I should remember?

TOM: I was valedictorian of our graduating class.

GLORIA: So?

TOM: I spoke at our graduation.

GLORIA: I didn't attend our graduation.

TOM: Oh.

GLORIA: And besides, I thought you were supposed to have been president of the Student Council. What's the matter? Can't you and Ernie get your stories straight?

TOM: That, too.

GLORIA: What, too?

TOM: President of the Student Council, too.

GLORIA: Oh, a real big shot in high school, eh?

TOM: Yes.

GLORIA: Well, Mr Big Shot, I do not remember those days. They've just completely slipped my memory.

TOM: What a shame.

GLORIA: For some of us, yeah.... When's he comin' back?

TOM: Who?

GLORIA: Ernie. You know, the person who lives here with me. When is Ernie comin' back?

TOM: Soon.

GLORIA: How soon?

TOM: I don't know.

GLORIA: He didn't tell you?

TOM: I don't remember.

GLORIA: You don't remember if he told you?

TOM: I don't remember what said when he told me.

GLORIA: My, my, what a short memory we have.

TOM: No shorter than yours.

GLORIA: A hell of a lot shorter than mine. *(Slight pause)* Okay, buster, okay. So what'd you do? Take a cab or somethin'?

TOM: I beg your pardon.

GLORIA: I didn't see your red Corvette outside.

TOM: I don't have a red Corvette.

GLORIA: Oh, you don't, do you?

TOM: Not at the moment, no.

GLORIA: Plan on gettin' your hot little hands on one in the near future, then, do you?

TOM: You might say that, yes.

GLORIA: *(To herself)* All right, Ernie, all right. *(To* TOM*)* Well, then, tell me. How's the folks?

TOM: Folks?

GLORIA: Yeah, you know, little Moms and Pops. The people you just happen to be stayin' with while you're passin' through on your way to college for the second time. How are they?

TOM: My parents are dead.

GLORIA: Is that so?

TOM: Yes.

GLORIA: You and Ernie, huh?

TOM: Yes, me and Ernie.

(Slight pause)

GLORIA: Listen, who the hell are you? Somebody Ernie just dragged in here off the streets? Or are you somebody he just dreamed up? Somebody he just dreamed up to try and keep me occupied, keep me distracted, keep me wallowin' around in this dump 'til he gets back from wherever the hell it is he's gone off to.

(TOM *smiles slowly.*)

TOM: You know who I am.

(Slight pause)

GLORIA: Yeah, maybe I do. Maybe I do at that.... You're at bogarter, that's who you are. A squatter, a spy, a trespasser on private property. And I want your snotty little ass outta here right now. I mean, what gives you the right to come snoopin' around wherever you please, to come bustin' in on people whenever and wherever you please? You think that just 'cause you're all rich and collegiate and refined and shit that you can have whatever and whoever you want? That I'm yours just for the askin', for the takin'? Is that what you think?

(TOM *says nothing.*)

GLORIA: Well, answer me, dammit.

(TOM *still says nothing.*)

GLORIA: What's the matter? Don't you hear me? Ain't you here?

(Again TOM *says nothing.*)

GLORIA: Why, you goddam stuck-up little—

(GLORIA *rushes to* TOM *and tries to beat him with her fists, but he grabs her by the wrists and holds them firmly. She tries to break free.*)

GLORIA: Let go of me.

(TOM *holds on.*)

GLORIA: I said let go to me, dammit! If you don't let—

(TOM *suddenly lets go.* GLORIA *backs away, rubbing her wrists.*)

GLORIA: You. *(Pause)* Yeah, I remember you. All of you. Walkin' around with your heads all up in the air or buried in those goddam books of yours. Always

makin' plans, always talkin' about college and your
future careers. Runnin' all the clubs, all the games
and activities. Runnin' the whole goddamn school....
Yeah, I used to watch you, watch little cliquish clumps
of you struttin' all up and down the halls and pushin'
me aside like I was nothin' to speak of.... Yeah, I
remember you. I remember the look and the smell of
you. I remember the…imagined taste of you in my…
in my mouth. *(She begins moving slowly toward* TOM.*)*
Yeah. Always wanted to know you. To feel you. To run
my hands all up and down your skin. To let you rub
whatever special thing it was that you had all over me
so I'd feel softer and gentler and much more refined.
*(She begins running her fingers through his hair and over
his face.)* Always wanted to make you…see me. Make
you…give it to me. Make you…give in to me. Make
you ….

*(*GLORIA *and* TOM *kiss passionately. The lights fade out on
them and a spotlight come up on* ERNIE.*)*

ERNIE: Yeah, I used to watch him back in school. Used
to watch him real good. Shit, I watched him so hard I
practically memorized the motherfucker. And then I
found myself recreatin' every last bit of him over and
over in my dreams. Recreatin' myself in my dreams.
*(He pauses, as though he has discovered something for the
first time.)* So you see, it's destiny. That's what it is. One
hundred percent destiny.

(The spotlight fades out on ERNIE *and the lights come up on
*TOM *and* GLORIA, *who are sitting in chairs waiting.)*

(A long silence)

GLORIA: So where is he?

TOM: He'll be here.

GLORIA: His time is up.

TOM: He'll *be* here.

(Pause)

GLORIA: Thought sure you were gonna be different. Thought sure you were gonna help me change things around here.

TOM: I can't help where we live, how we live.

GLORIA: Like hell you can't. You don't even try. Shit, what I needed was somebody who was gonna get me outta this dump, not somebody who was gonna just settle in. What am I anyway? Property? A piece of furniture? Some kinda utility included with the rent?

TOM: You could move out, you know.

GLORIA: Not on your life, buster. This is my place just as much as it is yours.

TOM: Then you can start hittin' the streets again.

GLORIA: Shit, you better back up, mister. 'Cause you got the wrong-assed memories about me. Always have. I ain't the woman you happened to have dreamed up in that nasty little mind of yours. I'm the one who happens to be livin' here in this dumpy little place.

TOM: I don't see what you squawkin' so much about. You ain't doin' too bad by me.

GLORIA: Worse. I'm doing worse…. After those first hot moments, after that rich, exotic smell of you wore off, everything became worse than it was before. Three steps forward and five back.

TOM: So what you want me to do? Change the fuckin' rules of the game?

GLORIA: Yes.

TOM: I can't.

GLORIA: Why not?

(TOM says nothing.)

GLORIA: Do you know what your trouble is? Your thoughts ain't big and bold enough to bust us outta this place. That's what your trouble is. You've got this tiny little brain, see. And inside there's this tiny little runway, where only the teensy, tiniest little thoughts can take off from. And then only one at a time. Mr Small Time. That's who you are. Mr Jiveass Small Time.

TOM: Just stow it, baby, okay?

GLORIA: Sure, Little Ernie. Anything you say, Little Ernie.

TOM: I told you not to call me that.

GLORIA: And what if he doesn't come back? What do I call you then?

TOM: You know who I am.

GLORIA: I know what I remember.

(Pause)

TOM: He'll be back. He's *got* to come back. We made a special deal.

(The lights fade out on GLORIA *and* TOM, *and a spotlight comes up on* ERNIE.)

ERNIE: When I'm in my car it's like bein' in my own private little world. White interior, bucket seats, bossed-out stereo C D player. A sleek, smooth, air-conditioned sound system on wheels. My own music and my own space. I was born to make my own music and space.

(The spotlight fades out on ERNIE. *Then the lights come up on* GLORIA, *who sits alone, waiting. After a moment* ERNIE *enters. He and* GLORIA *just look at each other for a moment.)*

GLORIA: Where have you been?

ERNIE: *(Irritated)* Out for a walk. Do you mind?

GLORIA: Don't go snappin' my head off. I was just worried about you, that's all. It's two o'clock in the morning.

ERNIE: It was too damn hot in here. I felt closed in.

(*Slight pause*)

GLORIA: I'm sorry I jumped so much on you earlier. Sorry I stomped out.

(ERNIE *says nothing.*)

GLORIA: It's just that sometimes you... Jesus, why am I apologizin'? Why do I always end up bein' the one to apologize?

ERNIE: I don't know, Gloria. Why?

(*Slight pause*)

GLORIA: He didn't show, did he?

(ERNIE *says nothing.*)

GLORIA: He never said he'd come here, did he?

(*Again* ERNIE *says nothing.*)

GLORIA: Did you bump into him at all on the street last week?

ERNIE: Man, do I wish I had me a car like his.

GLORIA: Ernie, you've got to tell me the truth.

ERNIE: Shit, all *I* could do for myself was walk.

GLORIA: Please.

ERNIE: Walk and walk and walk. Up and down those streets. Up and down, up and down, fuckin' up and down. Tryin' like hell to keep myself outta trouble, keep myself under control. Didn't even stop to rap to nobody. So afraid I'd go off. Go off. (*He looks around the space.*) Look at this.

GLORIA: What?

ERNIE: Just look at this.

GLORIA: Look at what?

ERNIE: And look at us?

GLORIA: What's the matter with us?

ERNIE: What do we do?

GLORIA: Lots of things.

ERNIE: I mean what do we *really* do?

GLORIA: What are you talkin' about?

ERNIE: Gloria, you bring on plates full of food and I take them off empty. That's what I'm talking about. That's what we do. We watch food appear and disappear right before our eyes a thousand times a day. Watch like hungry dogs beggin' outside the master's door. Servants in the big house. That's who we are. Servants in the goddam big house.

GLORIA: Honey, we do the best we can with what we got. That's what we do. And we are who we are.

ERNIE: Yeah, well, startin' tomorrow this man is gonna be doin' just a little bit more. Just you wait and see. And it's gonna be the beginnin' of our fuckin' climb outta here. You hear me?

GLORIA: Yes, I hear you.

ERNIE: It ain't always gonna be like this.

GLORIA: I know, honey, I know.

(Slight pause)

ERNIE: He just stood there. Lookin' all blank. Half-frozen in that tailor-made suit of his like I was gonna grab him or take somethin' away from him. Just stood there hardly sayin' a word as I talked, as I rapped on and on like a fool about those days at Central High. I was just tryin' to get him to remember, tryin' to get him to make some kinda connection with me beyond his, yeah, yeah, I finished college and shit. After all, we did go to the same school. We all did. And I do know a few things, you know. I ain't no damn dummy. But it was like it didn't matter to him no more. Like he just didn't wanna be taken there no more. Like he already knew that he had everything and I had nothing.

(Slight pause)

GLORIA: You got me.

(ERNIE just looks at GLORIA for a moment. She smiles. He half-smiles back.)

ERNIE: Where'd you go anyway?

GLORIA: Where do I usually end up goin'? Over Erma's.

ERNIE: Yeah. *(Pause)* You do believe me, don't you? About tomorrow?

GLORIA: Yes, I believe you…. About tomorrow.

(ERNIE and GLORIA stare downstage. After a moment a spotlight comes up on Tom somewhere in the space. Both ERNIE and GLORIA react slightly, although in isolation from each other. TOM smiles.)

(Lights fade to black.)

END OF PLAY

THE EXTERMINATOR

CHARACTERS & SETTING

OLD WOMAN, *white woman in her seventies*
YOUNG MAN, *Black man in his twenties*

A basement apartment in an American city

(While the stage is still dark, the chaotic sounds of people running and shouting and of windows and bottles breaking are heard. After a moment, the sounds fade out. As they do, the lights come up on an old studio basement apartment. U C—up center—is the one window that has dreary looking curtains, which are presently open. Just below the window is a small table on which sit several potted plants and a small radio. D L—down left—is an old overstuffed easy chair beside which is a floor lamp and an end table. On the table is a book, a pad and pen, and a pill box. U L—up left—are a sink, stove, small refrigerator, and floor cabinet. Just D L of kitchen is door to the bathroom. D R—down right—against the wall is a plain single bed. Just up from it is a door to a closet. The door to the hallway and beyond is U R—up right. A single chair is D S center. Beside the chair is a large box— closed and filled with books.)

(OLD WOMAN is U C by the window. She is wearing a housedress and slippers and is watering her plants as she speaks to them.)

OLD WOMAN: The light through this window is simply not bright enough for you to be at your healthiest. The water helps, though, doesn't it? It's certainly better than nothing, now isn't it? And if you'll just be patient, if you'll just persevere, I'm sure something significant will happen. Some new turn of events, some benign wondrous wind no doubt, that will whisk us away from here. *(She puts down the water can and looks out of the window.)* If only I could see more. If only there were more to see. *(She turns from the window.)* Well, I won't go out. That's for sure. No need for that. I'm sure there's nothing important, nothing special. Otherwise, there would be reports. *(She turns on the radio. She listens for a moment, works the dials. No sound at all.)* There, you see? Not a peep. *(Gesturing to the telephone on a stand near the front door)* And now the telephone is silent as well…. They've gnawed through, I'm afraid. Just gnawed right through. What nasty, inconsiderate creatures they are. *(Looking around the room)* It's the times, the times we live in. *(She goes to the overstuffed chair and sits. Then she takes up the book from the end table.)* Well, there's still the romantic view, now isn't there? It can still keep things at bay, now can't it? …If only my two fine young men were here. They'd know what to do.

(Suddenly, the eerie sounds of rats gnawing and scurrying about is heard. OLD WOMAN looks around.)

OLD WOMAN: Their sounds! If I could just rid myself of their sounds.

(OLD WOMAN puts down her book and opens the pill box. From it she takes some cotton, tears it in half, and stuffs a half in each ear. Then she takes up her book again and reads. The sounds increase as the lights fade to black.)

(After a moment the sounds fade out and the lights come up on OLD WOMAN asleep with the book in her lap. She begins to toss and turn and finally wakes up with a start.)

OLD WOMAN: Phillip! *(She listens for a moment. Silence)* Knocking. *(Silence)* Someone seems to be knocking. *(Silence)* Who is it? *(She gets up from the chair.)* Perhaps they're here. Perhaps they've come at last.

(OLD WOMAN goes to the door and opens it. YOUNG MAN is standing in the doorway. He is Black and is dressed neatly in jeans and a pullover T-shirt. He also wears brightly colored sneakers.)

(YOUNG MAN just stares uncertainly at OLD WOMAN.)

OLD WOMAN: I don't— Yes, yes I'm sure of it. Won't you come in?

(YOUNG MAN *hesitates and then comes in quickly. During* OLD WOMAN'*s next speech he first goes to the window and closes the curtains and then moves around the room looking at things.)*

OLD WOMAN: It seems like ages since I called. Ages. I can't quite remember when. Some time before the phone went dead, of course. Gnawed right through, you see. So you're just in time. Oh, I called so many times. And always the same answers, the same excuses, the same referrals. It was as though they had to wait for the right person to materialize. As though the person to handle my problem didn't yet exist. Until now, it seems.

(YOUNG MAN *simply stares.)*

OLD WOMAN: Well, how shall you begin? And what will you use? I don't see any tools, any tools of the trade. Not that I'm an expert, of course. Or even a dilettante, for that matter. Nonetheless—

YOUNG MAN: What the hell you talkin' about, ole lady?

OLD WOMAN: Why, the rats, of course.

YOUNG MAN: What rats?

OLD WOMAN: They're everywhere, it seems.

YOUNG MAN: So? I ain't into rats.

OLD WOMAN: But they're threatening to engulf me.

YOUNG MAN: Well, now I do sympathize on a certain human-to-human level. But like I say, rats ain't hardly my specialty.

OLD WOMAN: Then you're not from the city?

YOUNG MAN: Well, yeah, yeah, I live here.

OLD WOMAN: I mean the city government.

YOUNG MAN: No, uh-uh. Don't have no need for it, know what I'm sayin'? I figure if I can't govern myself then nobody can.

OLD WOMAN: Then why have you come? No one ever comes. So why have you?

YOUNG MAN: Well, that there is one bona fide, up-front question, ain't it? *(He begins to pace.)* Aiight. Let's just call it some sort of coincidence. Yeah. Let's just say that I'm walkin' by. Just passin' by, you understand. And I just happen to stop at this door. Stop and listen to all the vibes emanatin' from this door. And they tell me that there's this woman. This ole white woman on the other side. And she's dreamin' herself some powerful-assed dreams. Know what I'm sayin'? And I'm thinkin' that pretty soon one of them dreams is gonna open up this door and just let me walk right on in. So I be patient. Real patient. I just wait real quiet-like on the other side of that door. And like voilà. Prophecy! *(Slight pause)* Well, I mean, that's what just grew up in my head as the answer to your question.

(OLD WOMAN simply stares.)

YOUNG MAN: Aiight, aiight, let's try somethin' different then.

(During YOUNG MAN's next speech he both acts out the scene and continually circles OLD WOMAN, who tries to remain in eye contact with him.)

YOUNG MAN: Get this picture if you can…. I be in the supermarket, see. And I just be walkin' 'round and 'round and up and down lookin' at all the food. Just starin' and starin', makin' out like I'm gonna buy somethin' but am havin' a hard time decidin' what it's gonna be. Of course, you might just find me—if you pay special attention—spendin' a lotta time around the fruit, mostly 'cause of the grapes. Those I can just break off and pop into my mouth like nothin'.

And I can slip an apple or orange in my pocket. And sometimes I even get a chance to open a box of cereal or somethin', anything, anything at all, long's I can chew it up fast. And other times I just outright walk out with stuff under my coat. Things that can keep me goin'. Especially cheese. I like cheese…. Yeah, all that food. All those colors and shapes and smells. All that goddam food just beggin' to be eaten. And yet despite it all, just look at what all the hungry people do. Why, they be tearin' each *other* to pieces. Tearin' each other to pieces and eatin' each other up piece by bloody piece. Ain't that a trip! *(He stops his circling and just stares at* OLD WOMAN.*)* And so now my bona fide, up-front question to you is this: do you think I should eat you up?

OLD WOMAN: Oh, no, no, of course not. There's no need. No need at all. I've got food. I've stocked up. Would you like something to eat?

YOUNG MAN: How come you ain't scared of me? Most times white people be scared of me. Haven't you heard about guys like me who go around preyin' on ole ladies and shit?

OLD WOMAN: Well, I…

YOUNG MAN: 'Cause I have. Matter of fact, I know one of'em. Smashed her head in, that's what he did. Stole her TV and left her there conked out on the crackerjack floor.

OLD WOMAN: Oh, my goodness.

YOUNG MAN: Yeah, me, too. Terrible thing what this dude I know did. Terrible…. But that's not me. I'm not like him. Not at all like him.

OLD WOMAN: Then I shall feed you.

YOUNG MAN: Why?

OLD WOMAN: Because you're hungry. And because now I think I understand.

YOUNG MAN: Understand what?

OLD WOMAN: Why you've come.

(YOUNG MAN *thinks for a moment.*)

YOUNG MAN: Aiight, I'll sit, you feed.

OLD WOMAN: Wonderful.

(YOUNG MAN *goes D R and sits in the chair.* OLD WOMAN *goes to the kitchen area.*)

OLD WOMAN: And I do have your favorites, you know. Cheese and crackers, even grapes. I just happen to have them. It's providential, that's what it is. Providential…. Phillip, can you see? Can you see what's happening?

(YOUNG MAN *looks with a start but sees no one but* OLD WOMAN, *who brings a plate of cheese, crackers, and grapes to him.*)

OLD WOMAN: Here you are.

(YOUNG MAN *pulls the huge box around in front of him and then grabs the plate of food and sets it on the box. Then he eats ravenously.*)

OLD WOMAN: That's right. Use the box. It's only right that you should use that box…. Oh, how I remember now, how vividly I remember. And then several months after it happened. Phillip sitting so sternly in his favorite chair. "It'll be dark forever, Millie," he said to me. "I'm not sure I can live through that. Darkness forever. It's like the world has disappeared." "But your other senses," I said to him. "You still have your other senses. And you still have me." "But I can't *see* you," he cried. "Touch me," I said. "Touch me, Phillip. There's always touch. There will always be touch." And then I reached out to him. But when my fingertips brushed his arm he pulled it away.

(OLD WOMAN *reaches to touch Young Man as he continues eating but stops short of doing so.)*

OLD WOMAN: "Trust me," I pleaded with him. "Please trust me." "It's impossible, Millie, simply impossible." "What is?" I asked. "To have a view of the world, of life when you can't see." "Nonsense," I said. "The *fact* of life is all. The *fact*."...But it didn't help. Death was all he felt, all he claimed to see. The romance was over. He wasn't a violent man, you know. My Phillip. But he'd always owned a gun.

(YOUNG MAN *stops eating suddenly and turns toward* OLD WOMAN. *When he sees that she doesn't have a gun in her hand, he returns to his eating.)*

OLD WOMAN: So you see, I know all about suicide. Know it's never the answer. One must be patient. One must live through things.

YOUNG MAN: *(Continuing to eat)* Whole world crumblin' all around her and she wants to live through things.

OLD WOMAN: It's the only way.

(YOUNG MAN *jumps up, letting the plate fall to the floor.)*

YOUNG MAN: Hey, now hold up. You not poisonin' me or anything, are you? There ain't no poison in this food, is there?

OLD WOMAN: No, of course not. Why should there be?

YOUNG MAN: Well, you the one so bent outta shape about rats.

OLD WOMAN: Yes, but not you. Certainly not you.

YOUNG MAN: How you know? How you so damn sure? You already done made one mistake about me, you know.

OLD WOMAN: Yes, but now I know. And besides, distinctions must be made.

YOUNG MAN: *(Walking away from the spilled food)* Well, I don't want no more anyway. Don't even know why the hell I been here so long.

OLD WOMAN: *(Picking up plate and food)* Why, to see if I qualify. To see if I deserve to be rescued from them.

(YOUNG MAN says nothing.)

OLD WOMAN: You see, I, too, can be a preserver of life. I, too, can understand.

(OLD WOMAN takes plate and food scraps to the kitchen area.)

YOUNG MAN: Look, ole lady, if you think food is all I want, then you got another thought comin'. I need me some exchangeables, you understand? Some portable exchangeables. You not gettin' off this easy just by goin' off on me. I mean like I'm not livin' in your dreams, you know. I got my own life, know what I'm sayin'? I'm trippin' on my own brain waves. So don't be tryin' to drag me down none of your memory lanes. I don't remember, you hear me? I do *not* remember. I mean like we might be in the same crack and all, but that don't necessarily make me a part of your story. Matter of fact, as far as I'm concerned, *you* are a part of *mine.*

OLD WOMAN: A crack?

YOUNG MAN: Yeah, a crack. And not like cocaine and shit neither. *A* crack, know what I'm sayin'?

OLD WOMAN: I'm afraid I don't.

YOUNG MAN: Oh, you don't, do you? Well, then just listen to this.

(YOUNG MAN takes OLD WOMAN by the arm and escorts her to the chair.)

YOUNG MAN: Just sit yourself down right here, right in this seat of…nourishment, and listen to this here story of mine.

OLD WOMAN: But I—

YOUNG MAN: Sit, dammit, sit! Before I knock the…

(YOUNG MAN *abruptly lets go of* OLD WOMAN. *Then he composes himself by speaking to himself.*)

YOUNG MAN: No, man, no. You not him. Don't be him.

(OLD WOMAN *sits quietly.*)

YOUNG MAN: Right. Real right. *(He stands erect and faces D S. He clears his throat.)* "The Crack Story" by…by me. *(He tells his story in a very animated way.)* Once upon a time, back when I was a real young and inexperienced dude, I was gonna see this picture, see. This scary picture. I had checked it out on the sci-fi channel and I was gonna see it. An ole science fiction picture called *A Crack in the World.* 'Course, I don't remember what it was about 'cause I never did get to see it. But I figure I would've liked it 'cause at that time I really liked scary pictures and monster pictures and shit like that. Even those Japanese ones with their plastic dragons and cardboard sets and little Japanese people runnin' around twice the speed of sound and talkin' like their lips ain't connected to their brains. 'Course, a lotta the brothers at the home upstate couldn't stand those Japanese ones. Called them dumb and phony and ignorant and shit. But what the hell? Why get all bent outta shape about plastic dragons? I mean, the whole world's made up of plastic and cardboard and tiny little people runnin' around and bein' stepped on like they only half human, so it was like real to me. Only this time I wasn't in no home upstate. I was in this dude's apartment in the city. This dude who picked me up at the arcade. I mean, it's like survivin', know what I'm sayin'. Like doin' a little bit of this and a little bit of

that just to keep things goin', keep things movin' right
along. And this was real late at night and he was asleep
in the other room. And I was thinkin' maybe I oughtta
just say, fuck it, and put a big ole crack in *his* head.
But that don't happen, see, 'cause I fell dead asleep.
Yeah. Fell right dead asleep. And that's when I had this
dream about fallin' into this crack in the world, where
nobody could get me but also where I couldn't get out.
And I kept screamin' and screamin' and hearin' all this
roarin'-like activity upstairs somewhere. But nothin's
happenin'. I mean like nobody's comin'. So there I am
strugglin' and kickin' and dyin' from lack of food and
water and air when all of a sudden I just like pop open
my eyes and wake up. And that's when I see that the
picture was gone, yo. And some slick ole white dude
was talkin' at me 'bout Viagra like I was in the market
or somethin'. And I get so damn mad that instead of
turnin' off the TV like a civilized dude I up and kick
in the picture tube with my foot. And then naturally I
have to break ass gettin' outta there before you-know-
who wakes up.... So I missed it. "The Crack in the
World." But it don't matter 'cause just thinkin' 'bout
seein' it made me have this powerful-assed dream.
And that dream just happens to fit right in with the
reality of things, the reality of how people can just step
into places and be gone, be gone forever. (*He stops,
drained.*)

OLD WOMAN: What a wonderful story. What a
wonderfully romantic story!

YOUNG MAN: Romantic?! ...Were there any honeys
in it? Did I mention even *one* young honey? Even in a
cameo role?

OLD WOMAN: Why, no but—

YOUNG MAN: Then just keep me outta your head, yo. I ain't here for that. That was *my* story. You can't be claimin' it just like that.

OLD WOMAN: I know. I'm sorry. Still, it was wonderful.

YOUNG MAN: *(Blushing despite himself)* Well, I'm glad you liked it. *(Whirling around)* And now to show you just *how* glad I am, I'll just take me an honest-to-goodness portable exchangeable for my pains. Sorta as a reward for entertainin' you, for tellin' my story so good. *(He goes to the table.)*

OLD WOMAN: But what? Not my plants, I hope. Please, not them.

YOUNG MAN: Who the hell needs plants?

OLD WOMAN: They're important companions in these difficult times.

YOUNG MAN: Huh, they should be out in the jungle fendin' for theyselves just like me, yo.

OLD WOMAN: Still, you wouldn't—

YOUNG MAN: Naw, naw. I see what I want.

(He grabs up the radio.)

OLD WOMAN: The radio? But it doesn't work.

YOUNG MAN: Says who?

OLD WOMAN: I've tried many a time.

(YOUNG MAN holds up the radio's cord, the end of which is not plugged in to any socket.)

YOUNG MAN: Well, it ain't plugged in, ole lady. You try pluggin' it in lately? Or did you just guess?

OLD WOMAN: Oh, my.

YOUNG MAN: *(Heading for door with radio)* You got rocks in your head, ole lady. Boulders.

OLD WOMAN: *(Going toward* YOUNG MAN*)* But what about the rats?!

YOUNG MAN: Nonexchangeables.

OLD WOMAN: But something must be done.

YOUNG MAN: *(Turning around quickly)* Didn't I tell you to keep me outta your dreams?

OLD WOMAN: But they're not just there. They're everywhere!

(Suddenly, YOUNG MAN*'s demeanor and voice change. There's an air of sophistication and maturity about him. He stands very erectly and speaks very deliberately.)*

YOUNG MAN: Then pick up the telephone and dial for help.

*(*OLD WOMAN *senses that* YOUNG MAN *has changed and almost involuntarily participates in a kind of measured, ritualistic exchange.)*

OLD WOMAN: It's dead.

YOUNG MAN: Then go out.

OLD WOMAN: I can't.

YOUNG MAN: Why not?

*(*OLD WOMAN *says nothing. After a moment* YOUNG MAN *reaches out to touch* OLD WOMAN *but at the last minute withdraws. Then he smiles.)*

YOUNG MAN: Dream on, ole lady. Dream on.

*(*YOUNG MAN *turns, opens the door, and exits without closing it behind him. Meanwhile,* OLD WOMAN *moves slowly D S.)*

OLD WOMAN: He won't get far, you know. They'll throw this net over him or set this trap for him or feed him this.... *(Slight pause)* I did feed him food, didn't I, Phillip? I did "take him into me," as Matthew would say. I did do it. Of course, he wasn't really a scared

little colored boy this time. Not the way you saw him:
his eyes large and pleading, his nervous, ashy hands
outstretched. Not that way this time. They're Black
now. Nonetheless, I *did* do it. I *am* preparing myself.
(Suddenly rocked by another memory) "You're a fool,
Phillip McCauley. A fool for taking the nigger boy in.
Think about your wife, think about her." And then
I told you not worry, that I was fine. Told you to do
what you had to do. *(An even more painful memory)*
Oh, my God! Phillip, Phillip, what's happened?!
Your face is all bloody. *(Her arms outstretched)* Help
me! Somebody please help me! My husband's hurt!
They've hurt him! *(Her arms now raging.)* I hate you! I
hate you all! Your views are cheap, false, disgusting.
Just go away. Go away and leave us alone!

(The rat sounds begin again. OLD WOMAN *listens for a
moment.)*

OLD WOMAN: Do you hear them, Phillip? ...Who will
come? Who will come to save me? *(She turns U S and
gasps when she sees that the front door is still open. She
freezes for a moment. Then she goes slowly to the doorway
and stands before it. She makes a move to go out, hesitates,
and then closes the door quickly.)* No.... No.

*(*OLD WOMAN *turns and looks around the room. The rat
sounds have increased. She covers her ears with her hands.
When she catches sight of her plants, she drops her hands
and goes to them.)*

OLD WOMAN: You aren't the only ones rooted, you
know. You aren't the only ones firmly rooted. I have
my strength and sustenance, too. *(She goes to the end
table and takes up her book, holding it up for her plants to
see.)* I have my dreams, my memories. I have my view
of the world, too. *(She very deliberately and properly sits
down in the overstuffed chair with her book.)* I know what
sanity is. *(She puts the book down, opens her pill box, and*

gets more cotton. She puts some in each ear. She thinks for a
moment and then takes up her pad and pen and writes.) "A
world awash in goodness and light. A world bursting
with romance and chivalry." *(She looks at what she's
written and then puts the pad and pen back on the end
table.)* Yes. That should hold me for a while. I know
what sanity means. What it looks like.

*(OLD WOMAN takes up her book and begins reading. The
rat sounds increase further as the lights fade to black.)*

*(After a moment the sounds fade out and the lights come up.
OLD WOMAN is again asleep with the book in her lap. After
a moment more, the sound of someone trying to jimmy the
lock on the front door is heard. Soon the lock is forced and
the door edges open. YOUNG MAN comes in. This time he
is wearing cargo pants and an old sweatshirt that has been
turned inside out and has sleeves that have been cut short.
However, he is wearing the same bright-colored sneakers as
before. His hair is unkempt and his manner is more than a
little manic. He is much less together than he was before.
In fact, he will even have a bit of a nervous stutter in his
speech.)*

*(YOUNG MAN is so surprised to see OLD WOMAN that he
turns quickly to go and in the process inadvertently knocks
the telephone from the stand. She wakes up as he clumsily
puts the telephone back in place.)*

OLD WOMAN: Matthew? Is that you?

YOUNG MAN: Uh, naw, naw, it ain't Matthew.

(OLD WOMAN just stares.)

YOUNG MAN: Look, lady, don't panic, awright? Just
don't panic.

OLD WOMAN: I won't. Just tell me who you are.

YOUNG MAN: Uh…nobody. Nobody special. I just…
well ….

OLD WOMAN: I don't suppose you're from the city.

YOUNG MAN: *(Thinking)* Uh…naw, naw. Upstate. Actually, I'm from—

OLD WOMAN: *(With a sigh)* I didn't think so.

(OLD WOMAN and YOUNG MAN just stare at each other for a moment.)

OLD WOMAN: What do you want?

YOUNG MAN: *(Slightly at a loss)* Well, I was just…I mean like I just wanted to…. You got the time?

OLD WOMAN: I'm afraid not. Not at the moment.

(Realizing that OLD WOMAN is not in the least bit taken aback by his somewhat lame excuse for being where he is, YOUNG MAN pursues the subject more boldly.)

YOUNG MAN: Well, why not? Folks should know the time, you know. Watches, clocks.

(YOUNG MAN goes to the window and peeks through the curtains.)

OLD WOMAN: It's not important to me anymore.

YOUNG MAN: *(Still peeking)* I can't see anything.

OLD WOMAN: Look up.

YOUNG MAN: What kinda window is this where you can't see nothin'?

OLD WOMAN: You've got to look up. Beyond the stairwell.

YOUNG MAN: *(Turning from the window)* Nothing to see.

OLD WOMAN: Perhaps it's dark.

YOUNG MAN: I need me a watch. Watches important. You know the time, you keep your balance, yo. Heard somebody say that once…. Used to have a watch. A Timex. Ex-time. Smashed the shit outta it when it stopped runnin'. Smashed it into a million pieces.

What's the use? A broken watch ain't nothin' but an ole piece of hangman's noose stranglin' you by the wrist.

OLD WOMAN: Perhaps it could have been repaired.

YOUNG MAN: What? A million pieces?

OLD WOMAN: Before you smashed it.

(YOUNG MAN *considers that assessment momentarily.*)

YOUNG MAN: I don't know.

(*For a moment more* YOUNG MAN *is off in his own world.*)

OLD WOMAN: Is there something that—

YOUNG MAN: What stairwell?

OLD WOMAN: I beg your pardon.

YOUNG MAN: You said somethin' 'bout a stairwell.

OLD WOMAN: Oh. Out the window.

(YOUNG MAN *goes to the window and peeks through the curtains again.*)

YOUNG MAN: Oh, yeah, yeah, I get it. Basement apartment. You just a little ole white groundhog, huh?

OLD WOMAN: (*Incredulously*) A groundhog?

YOUNG MAN: (*Turning from window*) Hey, now don't be lookin' at me like that. It ain't *my* fault. I mean you *do* look sorta pale, you know. How long's it been since you been outside anyway?

OLD WOMAN: Ages.

YOUNG MAN: Just what I thought. I just said to myself: now there's a person that ain't been outside in ages. My thoughts word for word.

(*Beginning to pace*)

And now I'm thinkin', I bet she don't know how really tired I am, how really worn-out, flat-out tired I am. I bet she don't know that. And yet despite all these terrible feelings of fatigue, I'm gonna do her one "humongous" service by givin' her an update on the lay of the land out there, as a bonus for her being so unhysterical toward me thus far.

OLD WOMAN: *(Hopefully)* Do you mean news?

YOUNG MAN: Yeah, you could call it that.

OLD WOMAN: Why it's been ages.

YOUNG MAN: That's what I figured. So let's just say I'm here right now as your newsboy. Or rather, right *now* I'm here as your newsboy.

OLD WOMAN: I see.

YOUNG MAN: So here it goes. Item: one more piece of current event, yo. Title: Affirmative Action.

(OLD WOMAN *very deliberately goes to the chair and sits.*)

OLD WOMAN: Nourishment.

YOUNG MAN: Good. You did that real good. *(He delivers his news story with a good deal of nervous energy.)* They run around, yo. Run around lookin' into things, scopin' on things, checkin' things out. Then they start profilin', profilin' as best they can. A leg here, an arm there, the hair just so, the clothes like this or that. Their world. Make it their world so's they won't be so lonely. Then they buy magazines, know what I'm sayin'? Buy magazines like magic-assed mirrors. Like they be buyin' theyselves, how they see theyselves, or how they stone sure like to be seen. It's a trip, a real trip, this affirmative type action. They watch TV, go to the movies, go to parties, dances, clubs, just to make theyselves come alive, keep theyselves visible, see what I'm sayin'? ...So my advice to you is to plaster your walls with pictures of your choice—things you are or long to be. Brighten up your life with all these sparks of affirmation. That should keep you goin' for a while without you ever havin' to move one tiny goddam inch from that chair. Or wherever else you happen to be situated in this here underground bunker of yours.

(OLD WOMAN *looks around her at the walls as* YOUNG MAN *continues.*)

YOUNG MAN: Is that clear? Did I get it right? *(To himself)* Hell, how would she know? Chill. Just chill out. Get more personal. Connect, connect. *(Surveying the room)* Yeah. So you in this place, yo. And I see you. I see you here in this place. So I've got you down, right? Got you pegged. No escape from *my* eyes.

(OLD WOMAN *looks* YOUNG MAN *in the eyes. He's temporarily frozen, like a deer caught in headlights. Then he quickly averts his eyes.*)

YOUNG MAN: But as for me? Total cloud cover. Ain't nobody got me. 'Cause since I know how people do, I've learned how to deal with it, how to fight the shit off. *(Whispering in* OLD WOMAN's *ear)* Never sleep in a room with mirrors. Always smash all the mirrors wherever I be stayin'.

(OLD WOMAN *moves away from* YOUNG MAN.)

YOUNG MAN: And I buy all the wrong magazines. I sit in bus terminals, train stations, sit on broken-down park benches readin' all the wrong-assed magazines. And people just be starin' with their mouths all open 'cause they can't say, "Uh-huh, there he is, there he be, I see him, I know him." Can't never say that 'cause they don't know shit. And as for me, well, I don't need no damn affirmations, none at all, 'cause all it do is *fix* you and then give some jive-time the chance to nail you to his wall like you was some picture of the world he could own.

(Slight pause)

(OLD WOMAN *gets up from chair.*)

OLD WOMAN: Would you like some tea?

YOUNG MAN: Some what?

OLD WOMAN: Tea. I'll fix us some tea. Matthew used to like that. He liked it when I fixed tea as we talked.

YOUNG MAN: Do I look like somebody who drinks tea? I mean just take a good look at me, yo. Would I drink tea?

OLD WOMAN: *(Looking him up and down)* Well, to be quite honest with you, I'm not really sure.

YOUNG MAN: *(Very pleased)* See, what I tell you? Total cloud cover.

OLD WOMAN: Then perhaps some juice.

YOUNG MAN: Naw, go ahead, fix your tea. If you think that'll help you some, help bring things into better focus, go right ahead.

(OLD WOMAN *goes to kitchen area.)*

OLD WOMAN: *(Putting kettle on to boil)* Tea's good for you. Good for the nerves.

(YOUNG MAN *goes to the chair and flops down in it.)*

YOUNG MAN: Man, am I tired. I need me some rest. Gotta rest, chill out for a while, know what I'm sayin'? Understand how a dude could just wanna chill out a bit, let hisself down real slow.

(OLD WOMAN *just stares at* YOUNG MAN, *who continues without turning to her.)*

YOUNG MAN: Are you gettin' this or am I goin' over your head? 'Cause I always be doin' that—goin' over people's heads. That's what the counselors always used to be tellin' me. Soarin' like a black hawk over people's heads. Soarin' like a hawk. *(Dreamily)* Always wanted to fly, to fly high in the sky, to soar over everything, over all the dirt and trash and crap, all the hungry, dirty-assed people. Just glide over everything, over the whole goddam city.

OLD WOMAN: Yes, the romantic view.

YOUNG MAN: *(Shaken from his dream)* What?

OLD WOMAN: The romantic view.

YOUNG MAN: *(Indignantly)* Romantic? Were there any young honeys in that...

(YOUNG MAN stops abruptly. Both he and OLD WOMAN seem to be trying to figure something out.)

OLD WOMAN: You reminded me a little of my nephew just then.

YOUNG MAN: When?

OLD WOMAN: Just back then.

YOUNG MAN: No, I ain't.

OLD WOMAN: Just a little bit.

YOUNG MAN: You just tryin' to pin me down is all. Nail me to your wall.

OLD WOMAN: Like my nephew when he was younger just a little bit.

(Slight pause)

YOUNG MAN: You got a black nephew?

OLD WOMAN: No, not the color. The way, the way he used to dream.

YOUNG MAN: I ain't tell you none of my dreams.

OLD WOMAN: Such wonderful dreams Matthew had.

YOUNG MAN: What you think? That I'm outta somebody's dream or somethin'?

OLD WOMAN: He would say, "Aunt Millie, I've got this huge dream, but I can't fit it into my life." He could never quite fit his hopes and dreams into his life.

YOUNG MAN: What the hell you talkin' about?

OLD WOMAN: The way he talked.

YOUNG MAN: I don't talk like nobody.

OLD WOMAN: Something about the images.

YOUNG MAN: Nobody talks like me.

OLD WOMAN: It's the images.

YOUNG MAN: *(Quickly getting up)* No! *(Beginning to pace)* I heard myself on this tape once. This counselor taped this interview or somethin'. But I said, naw, that ain't me. What you think? That I don't know my own voice? It's just a trick to get me to believe I said all that…. And yet I did remember some of those words. My head remembered…. But I don't sound like that, I said. I don't talk that fast, that wild. I ain't like those other dudes, yo. I mean like we can't *all* be the same. So turn it off. Turn that motherfuckin' thing off, you white bastard. You ain't never gonna know me, so don't be tryin' so damn hard. *(He slowly settles down.)* I don't sound like nobody I ever heard. So you wrong.

OLD WOMAN: Still, I do remember you. From the last time you were here.

YOUNG MAN: I ain't never been here before.

OLD WOMAN: I've got it. *(Touching her head with a finger)* The memory's right here.

YOUNG MAN: When was I here?

OLD WOMAN: A day or two ago, I think.

YOUNG MAN: Somebody else.

OLD WOMAN: At first I thought you'd come to exterminate the rats.

YOUNG MAN: What rats?

OLD WOMAN: They're everywhere.

YOUNG MAN: Naw, musta been somebody else.

OLD WOMAN: You took my radio.

YOUNG MAN: Uh-uh, no way.

OLD WOMAN: I'm certain that—

YOUNG MAN: Another dude.

OLD WOMAN: It was you.

YOUNG MAN: No! *(He flops down in the chair again.)* Look, lady, I'm sorry. I don't mean to be scarin' you or nothin'.

OLD WOMAN: I'm not scared.

YOUNG MAN: I just need to rest is all. It's a trip out there. Real dangerous. Just let me rest here for a while, okay?

OLD WOMAN: All right.

(Sound of boiling water)

OLD WOMAN: Oh, my goodness, the tea.

YOUNG MAN: Forget it.

OLD WOMAN: *(Going to the kitchen area)* It'll be good for you. Hot tea with lemon.

YOUNG MAN: *(Beginning to fall asleep)* No lemon tea.

OLD WOMAN: Matthew loved lemon in his tea.

YOUNG MAN: Just rest....

(YOUNG MAN falls asleep. OLD WOMAN stops making the tea and just looks at YOUNG MAN for a moment. Then she goes to him from behind and stands. After a moment, she raises her right hand to touch him but stops short of doing so.)

OLD WOMAN: Poor Matthew. Poor devoted Matthew. Oh, he used to tell me all about you. How he would bring some of you home with him. How he would make his home your home. He was only trying to help, to be kind. But they became so upset, those others. Not the proper procedure, they said. Getting too carried

away with his work, they shouted. Accused him of all
sorts of indecent, horrible things. "It's not true what
they say," he told me. "They just don't understand."
"Of course, they don't," I assured him. But they let him
go anyway. Fired him. And he was only trying to help,
to further open his heart. A finger in a hole in the dike,
he was. A finger in a hole. And now... (*She again raises
her right hand to touch* YOUNG MAN *and again stops short
of doing so.*) His touch scared them, I suppose. He could
touch and be kind and that scared them. Where was it
coming from, they must have asked. Where was such
love coming from? (*Slight pause*) He's dead now, poor
soul. Dead and gone.

(*Yet again* OLD WOMAN *raises her right hand to touch*
YOUNG MAN. *This time she succeeds.*)

(YOUNG MAN *jerks awake.*)

YOUNG MAN: Who the hell...

OLD WOMAN: I'm sorry.

YOUNG MAN: (*Jumping up from chair*) He's gonna be
comin', seekin' me out.

OLD WOMAN: Who will?

YOUNG MAN: Wonderin' where I've been for so long.

OLD WOMAN: Who?

YOUNG MAN: But if I leave without.... Look, lady, I had
nothin' to hold on to, see. Nothin'. That's what he saw,
what he said. You need you somethin' to hold on to.
Somebody. So I joined him, moved in with him, made
myself a part of him. 'Cause he was a leader—*is* a
leader. And without a leader, without a few you's, you
can't survive out there. And now I gotta pay. You gotta
help me pay.

OLD WOMAN: How?

YOUNG MAN: Give me somethin'. I need somethin'.

OLD WOMAN: I don't have anything else to give. Just my touch.

YOUNG MAN: I ain't never took nothin' for myself, know what I'm sayin'? Ever. You gotta believe me. Couldn't never pin that shit on me. Never nail me to that wall. "It ain't my voice," I said. "I ain't never said all that." "Confessions," he said. "Confessions." "Well I ain't a dude that would say all that," I said. "Too fast for what I know about myself, my voice." So it ain't for me, lady. It's for him. He's the one.

(YOUNG MAN *begins searching the room.*)

OLD WOMAN: No, please, there's nothing you'd want. Nothing exchangeable.

YOUNG MAN: There's gotta be somethin'.

OLD WOMAN: The radio was all I had.

YOUNG MAN: *(Noticing the huge box)* What's in there?

OLD WOMAN: Books.

(YOUNG MAN *opens the box and takes out a few of the books.*)

YOUNG MAN: Books?

OLD WOMAN: Mysteries, romances.

YOUNG MAN: *(Throwing down the books)* Shit.

OLD WOMAN: I've read them all.

YOUNG MAN: A waste of time.

OLD WOMAN: They're important companions.

YOUNG MAN: Magazines, I told you, magazines…. Where your TV at? Everybody got a TV.

OLD WOMAN: It's in a shop somewhere.

YOUNG MAN: You mean you ain't got no TV?

OLD WOMAN: In for repairs. In for years.

YOUNG MAN: *(Whirling around)* I can't go out with nothin', dammit. It don't work that way, lady.

OLD WOMAN: I'm truly sorry.

YOUNG MAN: *(Noticing closet door)* What's in there?

OLD WOMAN: Memories.

(YOUNG MAN goes to closet.)

OLD WOMAN: Just memories.

(YOUNG MAN opens the closet door and all sorts of nearly unrecognizable junk falls out onto the floor.)

YOUNG MAN: What the hell?

OLD WOMAN: As I said.

(YOUNG MAN tries to close the door, but the junk is in the way. He kicks at it in frustration.)

YOUNG MAN: Goddammit!

(Suddenly, the chaotic sounds of people running and shouting and of windows and bottles breaking are heard coming from the hallway. YOUNG MAN stiffens but OLD WOMAN remains calm. After a moment, the voices and noises fade away.)

YOUNG MAN: *(With relief)* Gone.

OLD WOMAN: Of course, they're gone. They just drop dead like leaves from a dying house plant. Too many walls. Too much neglect. Not enough light…. Nobody ever stays anymore. Or even comes. *(Looking pointedly at YOUNG MAN)* Except you.

YOUNG MAN: Look, I already told you—

OLD WOMAN: It's in the eyes, you see. The eyes never change. *(Going to window and looking out)* That's the real trouble with being below ground level. No eyes. I can sit for hours watching. I can see skirts and dresses. I can see pocket pants and brightly colored sneakers.

(YOUNG MAN *looks down at his pants and sneakers.*)

OLD WOMAN: But no eyes.

(*Suddenly,* YOUNG MAN's *demeanor and voice change. There's that same air of sophistication and maturity about him that he displayed at the end of the previous scene. He stands very erectly, speaks very deliberately.*)

YOUNG MAN: Well, I wouldn't worry about it none. You just fell through a crack is all.

(OLD WOMAN *turns from the window and looks with wonder at Young Man.*)

OLD WOMAN: Oh, my God.

(*During the next bit of dialogue* OLD WOMAN *slowly moves D S and stares out as* YOUNG MAN *slowly moves toward the front door. Again, there is a measured, ritualistic nature to their speech.*)

YOUNG MAN: People are always doing that. Falling through cracks. It's the world, the way it's made up. I've been jumping from crack to crack all my life. Not too many people even seen me. Ain't been seen by too many people. Cry for help and nobody comes 'cause don't nobody see you.

OLD WOMAN: I see you.

YOUNG MAN: Same crack. But what people in cracks gonna do but step on each other's heads to climb out? So like I said, you're just in a crack in the world.

OLD WOMAN: I miss the eyes.

YOUNG MAN: Just step outside for a while. You'll see eyes. Too many of them. Everybody hungry, scared. Better stick with these kicks. (*Indicating his sneakers*) Stick right dead in here with these kicks. They're safer. (*Backing toward the front door and opening it*) A lot safer. A lot safer.

(YOUNG MAN *exits, closing the door gently behind him.
An instant later,* OLD WOMAN *turns around and sees that*
YOUNG MAN *has gone. She quickly turns back D S.*)

OLD WOMAN: *(Panicky)* Matthew! Phillip! Don't leave
me like this. Don't leave me alone with your memories
like this. *(She goes to her books on the floor and cradles
some of them in her arms.)* I've been trying. I've been
trying very hard. *(She rises slowly with the books still
in her arms.)* Once Matthew said to me: "Aunt Millie,
there's this one young black man whom I can't reach,
can't seem to touch. I've tried very hard. But he won't
keep still, won't let me touch him. Why, I've even
dreamed about him. His large, darting eyes daring me
to know him. His dark, impenetrable face laughing at
my ignorance. I call to him, reach out to touch him, and
he just disappears. Disappears from the dream. *(She
switches from a characterization of Matthew's voice to her
own voice. She speaks very deliberately.)* His elusiveness
threatens me, frightens me, but I won't, I can't, let him
go. He's all of them in one. The ultimate challenge.
Because I see the future in those fiery, glistening eyes
of his, I must reach him, touch him. I must take him
in to me. I must. *(Slight pause. She returns to being her
natural self.)* Such a romantic view he had. Such a
brave, loving, romantic view. Just like you, Phillip. My
two fine, heroic young men. Early deaths for you both.
Early deaths for you all. Too much of the world in your
heads, on your minds.

(YOUNG MAN *enters quietly and stands U S.* OLD WOMAN
senses his presence but remains staring D S. This time
YOUNG MAN *is dressed stylishly in a dark-blue suit with
matching shirt and tie. However, he still wears the same
brightly colored sneakers. He's also wearing sunglasses. He
has the air of sophistication and maturity that he has had
twice before.*)

(Suddenly, the rat sounds are heard again. OLD WOMAN *drops the books to the floor with a shudder and braces herself.)*

(Slowly, YOUNG MAN *comes D S to* OLD WOMAN. *When he is directly behind her, he wraps his arms around her. After the initial shock of his touch, she almost seems to settle into his arms. They begin to rock slowly from side to side, a motion that is initiated and controlled by him. After the rhythm of their rocking is firmly established, she speaks in cadence with that rhythm.)*

OLD WOMAN: I know you…. I know who you are.

*(*YOUNG MAN *reacts in no way to* OLD WOMAN's *declaration as they continue rocking with the eerie rat sounds in the background.)*

OLD WOMAN: And I want to love you. I want to love you so badly. *(After a moment and with a painful sense of resignation)* But I can't. I just can't. Not anymore.

*(*OLD WOMAN *and* YOUNG MAN *continue to rock for some time, the rat sounds still in the background. Finally…)*

OLD WOMAN: Phillip…Matthew. The romance is over. *(Declaratively)* It's the city! The *city!*

*(*OLD WOMAN *and* YOUNG MAN *rock side to side for three more beats and then stop abruptly. The rat sounds increase as the lights fade to black on the still figure of* YOUNG MAN/OLD WOMAN. *The sounds continue in the dark for a moment and then stop abruptly.)*

END OF PLAY

A BIRD'S EYE VIEW

CHARACTERS & SETTING

BACKBOARD, *Black male, about 40 years old*
HAWK, *Black male, about 30 years old*

The Time: Now
The Place: Ex-Urban Development

(While the stage is still dark there's the sound of wind swirling through trees, almost a whistling sound. It gets louder and louder, swirling and swirling, nearly like a tornado, until the sound of a metal object dropping to concrete pierces the wind with a loud clang, and a man's voice screams: "HOOP!!!")

(With that scream the wind sound abruptly ceases and the lights come up quickly on the disused remains of a basketball half court that's fashioned on one end of an old tennis court, its concrete still covered only here and there by the green clay. The basketball court consists of a pole to which is attached, "mounted," if you will, a Black man, about 40 years old. At first it might seem that he's on a cross of some kind, but he's actually sitting on a stand that's strapped to the pole. He is, in fact, a wooden BACKBOARD for a basketball hoop. But there's no hoop.)

(BACKBOARD shivers, shakes his head, looking down and around.)

BACKBOARD: This gots to be stoppin', man. Gots to be stoppin'.

(Suddenly the shadow of a bird, a hawk, flashes across the court. Then there's the sound of a hawk. BACKBOARD looks up, squinting.)

BACKBOARD: There he goes again. Always be …. Wait, hold up…. Is he…is he…?

(There's a fluttering of wings offstage right. After a moment, another Black man enters. He's about 30 years old and is, in

fact, a HAWK. BACKBOARD *is genuinely happy to see him, although this is their first face-to-face meet.)*

BACKBOARD: Yo, man, what's up? How you be?

HAWK: I'm good. You?

BACKBOARD: I'm, you know, "hangin'" in there.

(BACKBOARD and HAWK acknowledge the double meaning of "hangin".)

HAWK: Yeah, that's wassup. I just… *(Hiding his true motive)* I just thought I'd light for a bit. That is, if you don't mind.

BACKBOARD: Naw, naw, it's cool. We cool. Your first time.

HAWK: Sorry?

BACKBOARD: Landin' here. I mean, I've peeked on you flyin' around but—

HAWK: Really?

BACKBOARD: Yeah. I mean, I ain't got "eyes like a hawk," you know.

HAWK: *(Acknowledging the metaphor)* Huh.

BACKBOARD: But I can see pretty good still. And you sorta unique, different. Not straight crow. You got more color in you. Know what I'm sayin'?

HAWK: Yeah, I'm not straight. *(Another tack)* That is, I'm not a— *(Flat out)* I'm a hawk.

BACKBOARD: Oh, wow, for real? Hey, look, I didn't mean to be—

HAWK: No, man, it's cool. 'Cause I *do* see real good, you know. My eyes, they *exactly* hawk eyes.

(BACKBOARD and HAWK both smile at that.)

I *am* related to crows, though. We're sorta in the same family and all. But yeah, different.

BACKBOARD: Cool, cool.

HAWK: Anyway, there's not much prey around. Or trees. That's why I don't be landin' here much.

BACKBOARD: Humans, man.

HAWK: Yeah.

BACKBOARD: Although not too many around here lately. More their leavings really. They put up shit then get bored or mad or crazy or somethin' and all of a sudden...

HAWK: Yeah, well, soon there might be— *(Holding back)* Yeah...humans.

BACKBOARD: Although they don't go for huntin' birds much up in here anyway. They like the land creatures. 'Cause they can't be flyin' away from they buckshot.

HAWK: Tru dat. Although who'd eat a hawk anyway? I mean, what human, that is?

BACKBOARD: Wouldn't know. *(Without thinking)* You'd make a nice trophy though. *(Backing up)* Not that I'd want you to be—

HAWK: No, no, I know. But then eagles be the best for that. Although they got that endangered species badge of honor shit going on.

BACKBOARD: I know, right? Still, you look...well, you lookin' good. Like I said, different from...

BACKBOARD/HAWK: A crow.

(An awkward silence. Then...)

HAWK: How long you been up, uh, out here?

BACKBOARD: Mad long, man, mad long. Ever since the humans put up a basketball hoop on one side of their damn tennis court. Huh. They always say "hoop". Folks don't put *me* up. They put up a basketball "hoop." Assumption bein' that a board just naturally

comes with it. When it, *we* actually come *before* it. That
is, we're between hoop and pole. But they be sayin'
"hoop" like I don't count. But then I be sayin' the
obvious right back at'em: ain't no hoop in this world
any good without a backboard. I'm the backbone,
know what I'm sayin'? It's about the call of the ball, the
beat of the bounce, the angle of the bank shot, about
the rhythms, the jazz of the game. The backbone.

HAWK: Yeah.

BACKBOARD: *(Slightly embarrassed)* Sorry about all that.
My forever riff.

HAWK: No, it's cool. I can see you've got backbone.

(HAWK *seems to be checking out* BACKBOARD *more. Then
he looks away, slightly embarrassed, as* BACKBOARD *goes
somewhere else in his mind.)*

BACKBOARD: I miss him, you know.

HAWK: Who?

BACKBOARD: Hoop.

HAWK: Oh, yeah, yeah, I can see that, too. So what
happened to him?

BACKBOARD: Wear and tear, man… Plus some other
things. *(Not wanting to get into it)* Humans. They a trip.
They can be tearin' each *other* up as much as they do
the environment. I seen me tennis matches turn into
shoutin' matches and cookouts turn into curse-outs.
Balls and ladles and food and shit flyin' every which
way. And then the owner, some big executive at some
company nowhere near here, he'd always be on his
son's case. The boy was like mid-teens or somethin'.
With Daddy-o drillin' into him typical shit about
being a man. He loved to "engage" him in one-on-
one basketball. They call it "Horse," although ain't
no horses involved. Shoutin' about how the game is a

metaphor. And Hoop and Net and me be sayin' damn, man, chill.

HAWK: Net?

BACKBOARD: Yeah, man, every Hoop comes with his own Net. And visa versa. I mean like they go together.

HAWK: Oh, yeah, that's right.

BACKBOARD: *(Remorseful)* She gone, too. *(Back to the story)* Anyway, youngblood, he tries, but he ain't no good at B-ball. Hell, one time he came out to practice by hisself. Kept missin' jump shots. The long, the short, the top of the key. Every damn one. Net nearly busted out laughin'. So did Hoop.... He did make hisself some layups, though. And they felt good. Especially to me. But you could tell they weren't good enough for him. Matter of fact, he was pretty bad at tennis, too.

(Slight pause)

HAWK: So...Hoop. What happened to him?

BACKBOARD: Like I say, humans, man. You can always count on humans to be fuckin' shit up. Even after they done made you... There was these three white dudes, see. Like late twenties or something. Horsin' around. Playin' Horse, in fact. And only one of'em was any good. But they was only half tryin' anyway. Matter of fact, they seemed a little drunk. Shoutin' and laughin', jivin' around, trash talkin' and shit. Huh, pretendin' to be Black, "street." Callin' each other the "n" word and shit. Hell, I wanted to kick their butts, but you know.... Then one of'em brings out this pocket knife, opens it up and starts wavin' it around like he just got called out his name in some funky ole bar. And right away Hoop tightens up on me and Net starts to shiver. Knife dude wants to be recreatin' some championship game, the final moments. A damn re-enactment. So he closes the knife again and puts it in his pocket. Made us think that it's gonna be all good, you know. That we be good…. Anyway, they all set up for the score. A pass, a feint, a block-out. Then a short jumper and swish. Nothin' but net. They scream to high heaven. "Buzzer beater, buzzer beater. Championship, championship." I hadn't felt a thing but the pull of Hoop and that orgasmic ruffle of Net, but another part of me sensed what else was comin'. And sure enough, after some lame-assed dancin' and fist poundin', knife dude is up on this other one's shoulders, his damn knife out and open again.

HAWK: Oh, man.

BACKBOARD: They took her. Had their way with her. Raised her high. Then knife boy put her on his head like she was a damn crown. But she just drooped over a side. Limp. Knocked out. Then they left…. Hoop cried for days. Was never the same. The joyous sound of Net's swish was gone for him. For me, too. From then on balls thrown up and through brought us more pain than joy. A measure of the score taken away. After that, especially after folks left, stopped playin' B-ball here, even tennis, Hoop aged in a hurry. Rusted out real quick. Then one night I could sense somethin' was up. Screws loosenin'. Then all of a sudden this great heave from me like he was willin' hisself away. Broke free and smashed with this boomin' clackety-clank onto the court. Loudest-assed sound I ever heard. Hoop's primal scream. His last goodbye. Tore right through me. My heart, my soul ripped out…. He lay at my feet for a whole week before the ole caretaker found him. Looked stupidly up at me. Then carted him off with a head-scratch and a shrug. Trash heap, junk yard, metal scraps, "repurposed." Who knows?… Humans, man.

HAWK: I'm so sorry, man.

BACKBOARD: Yeah. *(Slight pause)* After bein' crazy with grief for a few days, I thought, alright, I'm gonna get through this. Gonna try to move on. Bigtime owner will just buy hisself another hoop. Attach it to me. Wouldn't be the same, but it'd be better than dyin' of loneliness and shit…. But then, well…

HAWK: What happened?

BACKBOARD: Wasn't bigtime owner. Was his son. Hadn't seen him for a while, and then suddenly there he is, walkin' this weird figure eight up and down the tennis court. Up one end, then down to the net, then along one side, then back along the other, then down to the other end and start all over again. Over and over and over. Sorta in slow motion. Almost made me dizzy. Not like he's drunk though, or even high. Just kinda…not there all the way. First in his head and then lookin' up to the sky. And it's towards dusk, sun just gone over the cliffs, air coolin' down. Then suddenly he stops. Sorta like he's thinkin', or has just finished up with some thought. And then he goes to this high brush on the far side of the court and fishes around. And he pulls out this ole hunting rifle. Carries it like it's a load rather than somethin' he's used to usin'. He comes back onto the court and sits right down under me, back against pole. I can see his head bobbin', his feet flat on the concrete, his legs movin' back and forth at the knees, first in unison, slowly back and forth, back and forth like it could go on forever. And then in opposite directions of each other, sorta knockin' but in silence. A silent, sad kinda knockin'. And rifle's just sittin' at his side, bidin' its time. Young man way down. Down walkin', then down sittin', then his right hand down and the rifle up. Knees grippin' the stock, fingers searchin' for the trigger. Him not wantin' to look, maybe thinkin' if he can't find it he'll be okay. But he ain't, 'cause he opens his mouth wide like a scream

and blasts a bullet right through. And I shake like hell
'cause pole's been nicked by that bullet comin' out
the back of that boy's head and ricochetin' on its way
to wherever, sorta like a bank shot gone really, really
wrong. Me and pole's vibratin' for a second while that
boy's just flat out dead. Blood and brains all over the
concrete, pole swimmin' in it.

HAWK: Damn.

(A strange kind of stillness comes over the space. Finally...)

BACKBOARD: It's the stillness that bothers me the most.
When there's no breeze. Doors and shutters stop
creakin'. Leaves stop singin'. Cicadas quiet down to a
hum. No trace of planes in the sky. That's when I feel
most alone, useless. And then I look up and see you,
or maybe look down first, catch your shadow. Then
look up at this speck in the sky like a beautiful curved
cross, glidin' easy-peasy. And it makes me feel better
'cause I be less alone, less lonely. Like I be soarin' to
heal my soreness. Somethin' like that, you know. And
then I think about reachin' you, stretchin' up high, like
the pole gets longer and longer until it catches up to
you, brings you down to me, you perched on my top.
Backboard and Hawk, earth and sky, bound and free,
forgotten and observed. Windswept, needy, hungry.
Still and silent as shit. *(Slight pause)* Just what I be
thinkin' from time to time.

HAWK: Huh...me, too. I mean...sometimes, to catch a
current, I just close my eyes, see nothing, stop caring
where, when, or how. Then I be goin' deep inside,
leavin' my cares, my hunger, my need to hunt, to suss
out prey. And then I be nowhere and everywhere all
at once. With myself and away from myself all at once.
Moving and still, high and low, old and new. And
sometimes when I "wake up," open my eyes, it's not
to hunt, to seek out prey. It's to see...you, fixed and

solid, carefree in your "fixedity." And if the light is
right, if the sun's behind me, you appear like a cross,
a bigheaded cross, with its shadow cast down on that
dirty green ground, which means if I was to swoop
down I'd have two yous on which to perch. One solid
in air, one hot on turf. Solid and hot. *(Pause. He is
hesitant.)* I...I know where Net wound up.

BACKBOARD: Wait, what? For real?

HAWK: Yeah.

BACKBOARD: You mean you seen her?

HAWK: I think so.

BACKBOARD: Oh, man, what, how, where? Why ain't
you tell me?

HAWK: I...

BACKBOARD: Come on, dude, out with it. Where is she?
She good?

HAWK: Sorta.

BACKBOARD: What's that supposed to mean?

(HAWK says nothing.)

BACKBOARD: Naw, naw, don't be clammin' up now.

HAWK: *(Hesitantly)* This crow I know, well, he's got this
elaborate nest. Like it's decked out to the max.

(Slight pause)

BACKBOARD: Net?

HAWK: Yeah.

BACKBOARD: How she look?

HAWK: Pretty tight, actually.

BACKBOARD: And you was gonna tell me this like
when?

HAWK: Right when you talked about how them boys cut her down. But then I got scared 'cause I'm a bird too and, hell, I've built a nest or two outta all kinds of shit and, and—

BACKBOARD: Just stop while you's ahead.

HAWK: Least she's back in nature. 'Cause you know rope and all—

BACKBOARD: Yeah.

HAWK: I mean even you...

BACKBOARD: Yeah, yeah. Hardwood. Oak. *(Slight pause)* Net. Oh, Net.

HAWK: Yeah. Dude done added a "s" and made hisself mo' nest.

(HAWK *smiles at his cleverness, then chuckles, which causes* BACKBOARD *to finally smile and chuckle. Then...)*

BACKBOARD: You know, I've never really had...Well, you see, Hoop and Net, they always had each other, the perfect pair. Made me feel like the odd man out sometimes. Always their support though. There to support'em, you know. To take the pound. So I'm not complainin' or nothin' 'cause I had me the balls, the call of the ball, beat of the bounce, angle of the bank shot. Had all those feelings, you know. The slam, the roll, the gentle touch. The smooth, silky birth of the score. That was my ecstasy. All kinda feelings up in me. Always been enough. Was...used to be...but now.... Shit, man, I don't know what, how I be feelin' sometimes, half the time. I mean, the soreness, the "beat-upness," comes with the territory. It be all in the game, game of life, you know. But when you all alone and that feelin', that need hits, it be like.... And then I look up, and suddenly I be leavin' this ole pole in my mind. Free... Free like you.

HAWK: I'm not as free as you think. *(Slight pause)* I
come from east of here. A sorta used-to-be east of here.
Back there I was...I had.... *(Slight pause)* I'd heard
about it happenin'. Rumors, gossip, flock talk. But
I hadn't been thinkin' that much about it. Much too
busy with my new .... Well, I was flyin' high, huntin',
sussin' out prey, when I first heard it. And from way
the hell out I knew somethin' was up. Heard the saw
even before I saw it. A sharp, terrible screeching sound.
One of those manmade sounds, you know. Alien. And
I immediately stopped glidin' and kicked into high
gear, buckin' the currents, furiously flappin'. Soon I
could see trees fallin', slicin' through each other like
so many pickup sticks. And by the time I got there
mine was down too. My tree, my home cut down to
the ground. Shattered. I screamed, man. Screamed to
high heaven. Then I shot straight down like a...like the
hawk that I am. But I was too late. My nest in pieces,
my newborns flightless, helpless, dead. And then I
glimpsed her in the short distance, streakin' through
the treetops to attack and then out of sight. And the
saws kept screechin', the man engines churnin', and
I...I panicked. I should have circled, searched for
her, fought for her, tried to save her from her futile,
crazy attacks, but instead I shot straight up in the air
and away. Left her in the lurch. Too ashamed of my
fear.... After that I let the currents take me wherever
they wanted to. I didn't fuckin' care. Told myself I was
searchin' for another place, another "habitat." Only this
time I was gonna be goin' it alone. No more matin'. No
more chicks. Only me. My own self. Soarin' and on the
hunt only for me. Just a bird on the wing now. Flyin'
solo, flyin' high and dry. And that's how I wound up
here. And when I first flew over this human "habitat,"
I knew there wouldn't be much prey to hunt. But then
I saw you. Fixed, focused. Like you was on guard.
A sentinel of some kind. I'd soar high over you, see

my shadow move over you, imagine you feelin' me
through that shadow. Weird shit like that. And when
those damn crazy crows would fly down to the court,
prance around like they owned the place, or like they
was auditionin' for a damn Disney movie or somethin',
I'd get mad jealous. Stupid jealous. Which like made no
sense. You weren't prey they'd be takin' away. Much
less a damn tree for me to light on, hang out in.

(Slight pause)

BACKBOARD: Damn, bro, that's so messed up. I'm super
sorry.

*(Suddenly, from U L there's the faint sound in the distance
of trucks traveling along a gravelly road. HAWK looks U L,
worried.)*

BACKBOARD: What's that? What's up?

HAWK: Look, I gotta tell you somethin'. Somethin' I
saw along the road miles from here early this morning.

BACKBOARD: What?

HAWK: It was like a whole caravan, man.

BACKBOARD: Caravan of what?

HAWK: Humans with equipment in long open trucks.
All kinds of equipment. Backhoes, excavators, all kinds
of stuff to tear down and dig up and slice through. I've
seen it before. Back when I lost my family…. They're
comin' for you, Back. For this whole damn place.
Gonna repurpose it, I'm thinkin'. "Re-develop" it. You
know, *their* take on nature. Take and take and then take
some more. Never know what they want til they stop
wantin' what they think they got.

BACKBOARD: So what you want me to do? I'm fixed,
bro. Got a fixed purpose. And I ain't choose this place.
I would have gone for a nice park, a playground, even
a crazy school yard. Not somebody's private preserve.

But here I've been. Here I be. I can't go flyin' 'round
like you, fleein' the coup, so to speak. That be only in
my dreams, bro, my fantasy. I'm not—

HAWK: I'll take you.

BACKBOARD: *(Not sure he's heard right)* Say what?

HAWK: I'll carry you away.

BACKBOARD: You buggin'. I'm attached. Old and
useless.

HAWK: No, you ain't.

BACKBOARD: I'm fuckin' attached.

HAWK: *(Looking around)* I'll find somethin', anything....
Hell, I'll peck you off.

BACKBOARD: Forget it, bro. Thanks for the heads up,
but forget it. I can't go. Just save yourself.

*(HAWK just looks at BACKBOARD for a moment, then half
smiles.)*

HAWK: So who are you all of a sudden? That dude in
The Titanic?

(BACKBOARD says nothing.)

HAWK: Look this ain't love, you know. I'm just—

BACKBOARD: Ain't it?

(HAWK looks away, embarrassed.)

BACKBOARD: Like I say, I been watchin' you, too. After
Hoop rusted out, came crashin' down and folks stop
comin' around to play ball. I just happened to look up
and there you were. Suspended, glidin' all smooth.
Lookin' different from those crows. More colorful,
more different colors. I took to callin' you Cool Breeze.
"There go Cool Breeze again," I'd say. And when the
sun was high, you'd sometimes seem to disappear,
get lost in it. I'd squint and sorta panic, thinkin' you
wouldn't be back, that you'd be burnt to a crisp. But

then out you'd come, bright against the white clouds or the light blue sky. And I'd sometimes imagine myself a rocket, shootin' up to fly with you, even past you, into the forever. Or maybe just back to bein' a tree or somethin'. Tall, mad-handsome, with a big-assed trunk, sturdy branches all out, and leaves for days. Make myself useful again. In nature.

(Slight pause)

HAWK: I'd build a nest in you. *(Suddenly embarrassed again)* On a branch high up, I mean. Start a new family maybe.

BACKBOARD: Yeah. And I'd be your cover, your guardian…. Fantasy, bro. 'Cause humans…you know how they be—

(Suddenly, the sound of the trucks traveling gets louder. BACKBOARD stiffens up despite himself.)

HAWK: Back?

BACKBOARD: It's too late, Hawk. 'Sides, I'm too heavy for you.

HAWK: Why don't you let me be the judge of that?

(BACKBOARD remains hesitant.)

HAWK: Please, Back. Let me try…try and help you soar. Soarin' to heal your…our soreness.

(The truck sounds continue. HAWK and BACKBOARD stare at each other. Then HAWK reaches out to unstrap BACKBOARD, who doesn't resist. As HAWK continues, he and BACKBOARD touch for the first time.)

(Fade to black)

END OF PLAY

ELSE

ELSE was commissioned by the Lower Depth Theatre Ensemble (Gregory T Daniel, Artistic Director) for The Pandemic Plays, a 10-Minute Short Play Festival produced online in the summer of 2020.

CHARACTERS & SETTING

NAOMI WARREN, *Black female, early 40s*
CAROLINE WARREN, *Black female, mid 60s*

The Time: 2020
The Place: Northeastern American city

(NAOMI WARREN *is in her old bedroom in the house she grew up in. She's a Black woman in her early forties. She peers at a framed picture of her father that she holds in her hands.*)

NAOMI: You squeeze your law journals into my head, and I play the meek little law clerk to your judge and jury. You seem to condemn me for not being. For all my "not-ness." And I want to cry out that I *am*. That I flow, I glide, I dance. I fairly ooze with life. But it doesn't matter. It's no matter. No…thing. I want to cut away from you. Far, far away. But I can't seem to. And in the end you win, always seem to win. A bold, in-your-face, formidable advocate. Torch-bearer, forger into the future. Charles Hamilton Houston, Thurgood Marshall, Phillip Allan Warren, some cry out! …A dream, Daddy. A recurring dream, a kind of nightmare. *(Setting down the photo)* Lost you a while back. Like maybe at birth. Or the crib. 'Cause you wanted a son, I think. I don't know. First born a girl. Then another one. Then another. But it's like you were blaming me. The "out-there one," you'd sometimes yell. That's me, see. Was me. Or you. One of us, both of us. Hell, I don't know…. Anyway, Phillip Allan Warren. Father, Dad, Daddy. What I want…what I need right now is for you to come, to be coming…. So that I can—

(There's a knock on the door.)

CAROLINE: *(Calling from the hallway)* Naomi…you in there?

NAOMI: Yes, Mama.

CAROLINE: Can I come in?

NAOMI: Yes.

(CAROLINE enters. She's a Black woman in her mid-sixties.)

CAROLINE: You gonna stay in this room all evening?

NAOMI: *(Glibly)* Social distancing.

(Slight pause)

CAROLINE: What you been doing in here?

NAOMI: *(Glibly lying)* Rehearsing my eulogy for Dad's memorial.

CAROLINE: Humph. If it ever happens. The stripped-down burial was hard enough to arrange. Even for somebody like him.

NAOMI: You could try Zoomin' it.

CAROLINE: I'm not gonna be Zoomin' nothin'. I ain't Aretha Franklin. *(Slight pause)* So where're you coming from this time?

NAOMI: *(Defensively)* That's your question now?

CAROLINE: I just wanna—

NAOMI: All over, Mom, okay? Is that what you want me to say? I've been all over for a long-assed time.

CAROLINE: Don't you be—

NAOMI: Sorry, sorry. *(Softening)* For a long time. If it wasn't for the travel bans and quarantines and shifting rules and on and on I would have made it to—

CAROLINE: I know…I know. *(Slight pause)* He wasn't supposed to go to that conference, you know. We were going to go away finally. On a trip. Just the two of us.

NAOMI: Where?

CAROLINE: South Africa. Had it all planned. Three
precious weeks alone together, away from folks,
away from the clamor, the constant phone calls,
text messages, urgent emails. Counselor Warren,
please, please, do this, do that…. Was gonna be like
a new beginning for us, a kind of recommitment,
after so much…. But then one of his colleagues has
a heart attack and he has to fill in because, well, he
is who he is…was…. He got it there, they think. At
the conference. Lotta folks did. `Cause folks didn't
know. They, we didn't…weren't told, warned…. And
they brought it back with'em, back to wherever they
were from, spreading it, spraying it. And your father,
what with his high blood pressure and rising A1c….
(Building to a fever pitch) And he starts losing his taste.
Suddenly couldn't taste my potato salad, thought
something was wrong with it but I kept telling him
that it was all right…. And then some aches and pains
and this high fever and then shortness of breath and,
and before I can, we can…. That is, he collapses in the
den and I call 911 and they take him away and, and I
can't be with him, can't hold him, touch him, kiss him.
Not me, not your sisters when they rushed home. Not
anybody. With all those nurses and doctors in space
suits, body armor. Machines buzzin', tubes snakin',
pumpin', everybody rushin' here and there. And so all
I can do then, all I can do is whisper through the glass,
my breath against the glass, whisper "I'm sorry" and
"Keep the faith, Phil" and "I love you, love you, love
you." My hand touching, pushing at the glass, wanting
to just break through….And then early the next day, a
call like a thunderclap….

NAOMI: Oh, Mama….

CAROLINE: The strangest thing, though, the strangest
thing is that I am negative. I've tested negative. He
brought it back with him, carried it in him but didn't

pass it on to me. And I've been asking myself, "why?" What does that say about us, about what we've been through together? All these years of sharing, of being together, loving each other, caressing, comfort, care. Even with him away so much, traveling, advocating, and that slip up with that woman, on the road. And then contrite because we loved each other, needed each other. And I welcomed him home, you know. I swear I did. With open arms. Hugged and kissed him. Because we had plans, see. Had this trip all planned. A renewal, a blessed renew....

(Slight pause)

NAOMI: Maybe, Mama...maybe it was Daddy's last gift to you. When he held you last. Maybe his sonorous spirit was silently declaring: "No, uh-uh. Don't you dare. Not her. No."

(Slight pause)

CAROLINE: *(Half wistfully)* "No." ...Now that was *your* favorite word growing up.

NAOMI: I know.

(CAROLINE and NAOMI laugh at the odd word convergence.)

CAROLINE: Your Grandma Estelle used to say to me: "That's what you get for giving that child a name with a "N" and a "O" so close together in it.

NAOMI: Yeah. I used to run in here and slam the door behind that "no," too.... Stay out, I'd yell to Keisha and Pam. Y'all got your own room. This one is *mine*. Never mind the fact that their room was one they had to share. And then I'd curl up in here with my things, my books, my diary. Curl on up. Read, think, plan. Right up in here.

CAROLINE: That is, until you sprung on outta here. Eighteen and away you went. And not to Spelman or

Howard. To Pomona College, a place we'd never even heard of, all the way out in California. Way out and beyond. And then afterwards off to here, there, and who knows where.

NAOMI: It's who I was, Mama…who I am.

CAROLINE: No doubt. Meanwhile, your daddy insisted on keeping this room pretty much the same. As you can see.

NAOMI: Daddy?

CAROLINE: Oh, yeah. What? You think it was me? Uh-uh.… 'Course he never said it out loud. And folks have stayed up in here from time to time. Especially the boys. Your nephews. The wreckin' crew I sometimes call'em. But your daddy always cleaned up after'em. Or had Maria do it.… I'm still paying her, by the way. Maria. Even though she can't, shouldn't come over right now. It's the least I can do.

NAOMI: Daddy doing housework. Imagine that.

(Slight pause)

CAROLINE: You know, he stopped being angry at you for dropping out of law school years ago. He just couldn't admit it, say it out loud. And he didn't even care all that much that you never seemed to want settle down anywhere, with anybody. Long-term, I mean. Neither have I…much.

NAOMI: Mama, I—

CAROLINE: But what, Naomi? What have you been looking for all this time?

NAOMI: I don't know. Something, something…else.

CAROLINE: Meaning not this. Not us.

NAOMI: *No*, that's not what I mean. I— It's not either/or, Mama. It's never been either/or.

(Slight pause)

CAROLINE: Well, it don't matter all that much now 'cause I'm thinking about selling the house, putting it on the market.

NAOMI: Now? During all of this?

CAROLINE: This won't last forever.

NAOMI: Says who?

CAROLINE: Your idiot President.

NAOMI: Seriously, Mama—

CAROLINE: I *am* being serious. It'd be too much for me, this house. Too much emptiness. Too much upkeep. Besides, your dad was the entertainer, you know. The gatherer of folks, the filler-upper, so to speak. I'll...I'll buy a condo on the water maybe. One with a balcony so I can look out, walk out, feel the breeze, the waves lapping, the sun rising or setting. *(Almost to herself)* Make this life more about me maybe.

NAOMI: But what about Keisha and Pam, their families?

CAROLINE: They got their own houses. Their own lives....Yes, indeed. Sell this house, downsize, and maybe use the extra cash to help some folks out, 'cause so many of us are hurting now, in great need now. So why keep money I don't need tied up in this house? Meanwhile, I might donate your daddy's papers and such to Howard or the African American History Museum. I don't know. This is too big a place for me to be feeling so closed in.

NAOMI: No, Mama, no.

CAROLINE: There you go again with your "no".

NAOMI: Please, please, don't. Don't sell this house, don't move, don't leave.

CAROLINE: But it's *my* house.

NAOMI: I'll stay.

CAROLINE: Say what?

NAOMI: I'll stay.

CAROLINE: *(Half laughing)* Where? In this room?

NAOMI: In this house. With you.

(NAOMI suddenly takes CAROLINE's hands in hers. CAROLINE tries to break away but NAOMI won't let her go.)

CAROLINE: No touching yet.

NAOMI: Yes.

CAROLINE: No.

NAOMI: Yes! It's just my hands, Mama. *Our* hands. My clean hands in your clean hands.... You, we can still give, try to help out. But I wanna stay. See it through with you.... What I'm saying is that right now, right here: this is my...*this* is my "else".

(CAROLINE and NAOMI stare at each other longingly and either do or don't hug each other tightly.)

END OF PLAY